Romantic
Virginia

VIRGINIA IS for Lovers.

Now we are Virginians.

2013

Romantic Virginia

MORE THAN 300 THINGS TO DO FOR SOUTHERN LOVERS

ANDREA SUTCLIFFE

JOHN F. BLAIR, PUBLISHER   WINSTON-SALEM, NORTH CAROLINA

Published by John F. Blair, Publisher

COVER CREDITS—

Front cover: *Governor's Place Garden, Williamsburg*
Back cover: left, *Skyline Drive looking toward Stony Man Peak*
Back cover: right, *Sand dunes along the Virginia Beach shore*

International Standard Serial Number 1542-4669

ORIGINAL SERIES DESIGN BY ANNE RICHMOND BOSTON
COMPOSITION BY DEBRA LONG HAMPTON

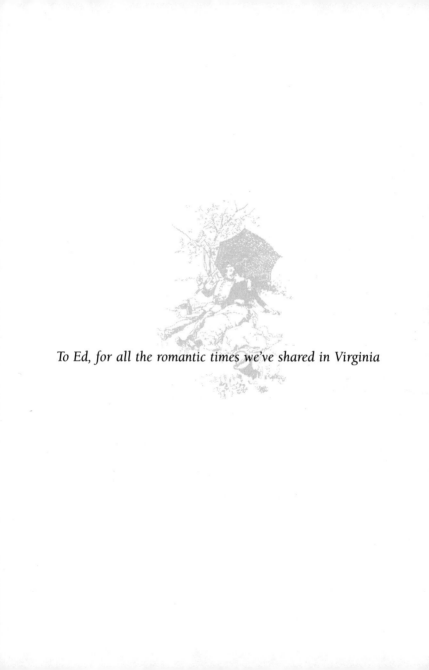

To Ed, for all the romantic times we've shared in Virginia

Contents

Virginia

SHENANDO

Roan

Radford

SOUTHWESTERN

• Abingdon

Bristol•

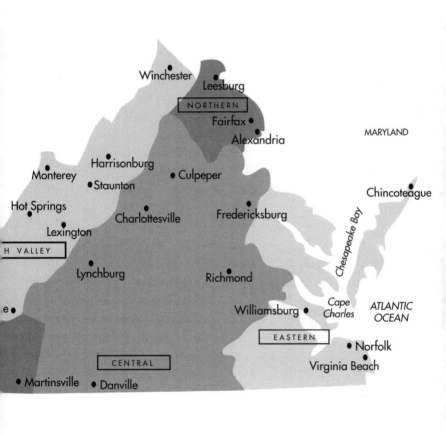

Winchester

Leesburg

NORTHERN

Fairfax

Alexandria

MARYLAND

Harrisonburg

Culpeper

Monterey

Staunton

Chincoteague

Hot Springs

Charlottesville

Fredericksburg

Chesapeake Bay

Lexington

H VALLEY

Lynchburg

Richmond

Cape
Charles

ATLANTIC
OCEAN

e

Williamsburg

EASTERN

Norfolk

CENTRAL

Virginia Beach

Martinsville

Danville

Acknowledgments For the past year, while combing the state for romantic places and activities, I've asked almost everyone I've met to tell me about their favorite spots. A few people went the extra mile, and I'd like to thank them here: Tom Orlowski, Peggy and John Roethel, Kathleen Sullivan, Jeannie Phifer, Erena Hunsicker, Jacquie Colligan, Julie Pastor, and Caroline Kettlewell.

Introduction For more than three decades, the state tourism office has declared that "Virginia is for lovers." This often-imitated slogan has an interesting origin. As first conceived, there were to be several slogans; ads would run with headings like "Virginia is for history lovers," "Virginia is for beach lovers," and "Virginia is for mountain lovers." But the decision was made to drop the modifiers and use one phrase instead of many. In doing so, the meaning got turned around a bit, with the emphasis on the lovers themselves.

Either way you read it, the slogan rings true—there is much for lovers to love about Virginia, for the very reasons the creators of the original phrases had in mind. This beautiful and diverse state offers something for everyone and every interest—historic sites, beaches, rivers, valleys, mountains, gardens, sports, music, the arts, good food and wine, charming places to stay, and more. The purpose of this book, unlike other Virginia travel guides that focus on family travel, is to offer a hand-picked selection of activities, destinations, restaurants, and lodgings that will especially appeal to couples.

Most travel guides are organized by geographic destination. Again, this book is different. To help couples find their favorite things to do, I have organized *Romantic Virginia* by activity and then, within each activity, by geographic location. Icons identify each attraction's location in one of the state's five regions:

Northern Virginia

Eastern Virginia

Central Virginia

The Shenandoah Valley

Southwestern Virginia

Then, within each section, the places or activities are generally arranged from north to south. The map on pages 10-11 defines the five regions and their icons.

To help couples plan a trip—whether for a day or a week— I've included "Romantic Getaway" sidebars for 14 Virginia cities or regions. These sidebars list ideas and suggestions for places to see, stay, and eat. Most are described in the book's main sections, but here and there, I've added a few other options. For example, I've included restaurants that did not make the cut as destinations for a romantic meal but that otherwise are top choices for lunch or dinner.

So what exactly do I mean by *romantic*? Well, romantic is more than what appeals to starry-eyed honeymooners. The definition for this book is broader.

First, romantic means being truly together—alone at last!— away from jobs, children, parents, even friends. It can be an evening out at an elegant restaurant, with candles and a linen tablecloth, where the two of you can focus on each other for a change. It can be an afternoon spent sampling wines at one of Virginia's many wineries. It can be a weekend at a small inn or bed-and-breakfast, where you sleep late and (at a reasonable hour) your host serves you a four-course breakfast in an antique-filled dining room or on a garden patio. It can be hiking hand in hand through the woods to a waterfall. It can be learning something new together at a history or science museum. It can be buying a painting at an art show or gallery or admiring great art together in one of the state's art museums. It can be getting married at one of Virginia's many romantic old homes or gardens.

Second, romantic means nostalgic—taking a long, loving look into the past. It's imagining the first settlers toughing out the winter at Jamestown, or picturing Thomas Jefferson sipping Virginia's first wines in his dining room at Monticello. It can also mean reliving your own past, by getting car-hop service at one of the state's surviving drive-in restaurants, slurping down an ice-cream soda at an old-time pharmacy fountain, or putting your arm around your sweetheart at a drive-in theater.

Third, romantic means just plain having fun. In Virginia in the summertime, for instance, you can spread out a blanket, sit on the lawn, and enjoy an amazing variety of musical and theatrical performances: country, classical, rock-and-roll, jazz, rhythm-and-blues, opera, and even Shakespeare. If the bugs bother you and the weather isn't right, you can reserve a good seat inside one of the state's fine theaters or music halls, from Alexandria to Richmond, from Roanoke to Norfolk. Romantic fun can also mean tubing down a river, skiing a slope, swinging at a golf ball, cheering on your favorite minor-league baseball team, soaring in a hot-air balloon, or watching a college football game on a perfect Virginia fall day.

Finally, romantic means going out and doing something completely different. If you've never gone whitewater rafting, sailed on a tall ship, walked through an old-growth forest, or tapped your feet to bluegrass music in an old country store, then why not try? If you do it together, you'll double the fun, and that is truly romantic.

I hope this book gives you plenty of ideas to launch a romantic adventure of your own. Have a great time!

HAVE I LEFT OUT YOUR FAVORITE THING TO DO IN VIRGINIA?

Because *Romantic Virginia* is intended to be an idea book, not an encyclopedic reference to all that's available in Virginia, I have provided, at the bottom of the 14 "Romantic Getaway" sidebars, contact information for visitor bureaus in the major cities and regions. For a wealth of information statewide, contact the Virginia Tourism Corporation at 901 East Byrd Street, Richmond, VA 23219. You may call them at 800-VISIT VA (800-847-4882) or 804-786-2051 or send an e-mail to VAinfo@virginia.org; its website is www.virginia.org. The Virginia Tourism Corporation distributes detailed information on outdoor activities, sports, dining, lodging, historic sites, arts, shopping, special events, wineries, and more. It also publishes 21 free travel brochures and booklets, including a scenic-roads map and the annual *Virginia Is for Lovers Travel Guide*. You can order these publications by phone, e-mail, or the Internet.

I've tried to ensure that the information in this book is as accurate and up to date as possible. I've also tried to list only those establishments and attractions that have been around for a good while and are likely to be here in the future. But keep in mind that things can and will change, so it's always a good idea to verify information with a phone call or website visit before leaving the house. I'd appreciate hearing about any changes you find so that I can make corrections in future editions of this book. And I've undoubtedly missed one or more of your favorite romantic spots or activities in Virginia. If you have suggestions for the next edition, please contact me at—

Romantic Virginia

c/o John F. Blair, Publisher
1406 Plaza Drive
Winston-Salem, NC 27103-1470
www.blairpub.com

Romantic
Virginia

*Arts
for the
Heart*

*Nobody sees a flower—really—it is so small—we haven't time—
and to see takes time, like to have a friend takes time.*

Georgia O'Keeffe, artist

There is nothing romantic, really, about sitting in front of the television. Why not get out of the house and experience the fun and excitement of music, drama, and art firsthand? Life is much more stimulating that way. Virginia is chock-full of all kinds of events and shows year-round; many are probably going on right in your area.

In the summer, you can pack a picnic and groove to music on the lawn under the stars. In the winter, you can attend a Christmas concert of your local symphony or see a Broadway play. In the spring, you can find out what opera is all about at a performance by one of the state's several opera companies. When was the last time you and your love saw a live Shakespeare performance? (Never, you say?) There are several troupes performing throughout the state. And on rainy days, forget the mall and the movie theater—it's less expensive and a lot more interesting to visit an art museum together.

MUSIC

Concerts at the Old School in Waterford
Waterford Foundation, P.O. Box 142 / Waterford / 20197
540-882-3018

Four seasonal concerts showcase a variety of musical talent. Past performances have included finalists from Metropolitan Opera auditions, chamber-music ensembles, choral music, and piano soloists. A bonus is the free guided walking tour of this historic little village given before each concert.

Bluemont Concert Series
P.O. Box 208 / Leesburg / 20178
703-777-6306
www.bluemont.org

Music, country dancing, and other special community events are offered throughout northwestern and central Virginia year-round.

Loudoun Symphony
P.O. Box 4478 / Leesburg / 20177
703-771-8287
www.loudounsymphony.org

Founded in 1990, the Loudoun Symphony performs five regular concerts from October through May. It also offers concerts in surrounding towns, including summer outdoor concerts in the Bluemont Concert Series in Leesburg.

The Filene Center and The Barns at Wolf Trap
Wolf Trap Foundation for the Performing Arts
1624 Trap Road / Vienna / 22182
703-255-1860
www.wolf-trap.org

The Filene Center, just west of the Capital Beltway off I-66 near Washington, D.C., hosts more than 90 performances in the summer months at this venue maintained by the National Park Service. Seating under cover is available, but it's more fun to bring a blanket and spread out on the lawn above the stage. All kinds of music, from symphonies to jazz to rock-and-roll, are performed here. Other musical and dramatic events are held year-round indoors in The Barns at Wolf Trap. The Wolf Trap Opera Company offers performances in the summer months.

 Fairfax Symphony Orchestra
4024 Hummer Road / Annandale / 22003
703-642-7200
www.fairfaxsymphony.org

The Fairfax Symphony performs its seven-concert MasterWorks Series at George Mason University's Center for the Arts in Fairfax. It offers free summer performances at Mason District Park in Annandale. It also performs pops and classical music over two July weekends at the Shenandoah Valley Music Festival in Orkney Springs; see page 11 for details.

 Alexandria Symphony Orchestra
109 North Henry Street / Alexandria / 22314
703-548-0885
www.alexsym.org

The Alexandria Symphony presents five classical and pop performances each season, between September and May, in the

Rachel M. Schlesinger Concert Hall and Arts Center at Northern Virginia Community College's Alexandria campus.

 **The Birchmere**
3701 Mount Vernon Avenue / Alexandria / 22305
703-549-7500
www.birchmere.com

Still a favorite of stars who performed here early in their careers (for example, Lyle Lovett, Vince Gill, the Dixie Chicks, and Mary Chapin Carpenter), this concert hall seats 500 for dinner and music. After 30 years, the place is a legend in its own time. The Birchmere showcases acoustic music and singer-songwriters of all kinds.

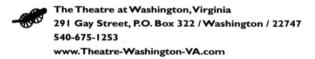 **The Theatre at Washington, Virginia**
291 Gay Street, P.O. Box 322 / Washington / 22747
540-675-1253
www.Theatre-Washington-VA.com

A variety of musical events, from chamber music to jazz, is held here on weekends throughout the year. Professional and amateur dramatic productions are also performed.

 **Virginia Opera**
160 East Virginia Beach Boulevard / Norfolk / 23510
757-627-9545
www.vaopera.org

Operas are presented October through May in Norfolk's Harrison Opera House, as well as in Richmond and Fairfax.

The Virginia Symphony
880 North Military Highway / Norfolk / 23502
757-892-6366
www.virginiasymphony.org

The symphony offers more than 130 performances from September to July in Norfolk's Chrysler Hall and several other venues in the region.

Jeanne & George Roper Performing Arts Center
340 Granby Street / Norfolk / 23510
757-822-1450

Tidewater Community College renovated this 1926 movie and vaudeville palace known as "the Lowe's." It is now used for arts performances of all kinds. The Jazz on Granby concert series is held here.

Verizon Wireless Virginia Beach Amphitheater
3550 Cellar Door Way / Virginia Beach / 23456
757-368-3000
www.verizonwirelessamphitheater.com

Popular music concerts are held in this outdoor pavilion—which has both covered seats and lawn seating—from May through October. Shuttle buses run from the beach area to this inland theater a few miles away.

The Ash Lawn Opera Festival
1941 James Monroe Parkway / Charlottesville / 22902
434-293-4500
www.ashlawnopera.org

This outdoor summer opera festival takes place in the gardens of Ash Lawn-Highland, home of President James Monroe.

A nationally recognized summer musical event, it's been going on for more than 25 years now. Besides opera, the festival includes Music at Twilight, a five-concert series of classical and contemporary music.

Wintergreen Summer Music Festival
Wintergreen Performing Arts, Inc., P.O. Box 816 /
    Nellysford / 22958
434-325-8292
www.wtgmusic.org

Visitors can enjoy orchestral music under the stars at Wintergreen Resort all summer long.

highlight

Charlottesville Loves a Song, a Dance, a Play, and a Poem . . .

Musical events take place almost daily in Charlottesville. For a weekly listing, visit www.charlottesvillemusic.com. A good source of information on cultural events, provided by the Piedmont Council of the Arts, is ArtsLine, which may be reached at 434-977-4177 for schedule and ticket information.

Richmond Symphony
   Orchestra
300 West Franklin Street /
   Richmond / 23220
800-788-1437 or 804-788-1212
www.richmondsymphony.com

The Richmond Symphony puts on more than 40 classical, pops, and baroque concerts a year in various venues, including the Carpenter Center and the Landmark Theatre. It offers free summer concerts at Pocahontas State Park

Lynchburg Symphony
   Orchestra
621 Court Street / Lynchburg /
   24504
434-845-6604
www.lynchburgva.com/
   symphony

The Lynchburg Symphony has been bringing live classical music to central Virginia since 1983. It offers a year-round schedule of concerts and ensembles, including a Christmas concert and an outdoor summer pops concert.

Shenandoah Summer Music Theatre
Ohrstrom-Bryant Theatre, Shenandoah University,
1460 University Drive / Winchester / 22601
877-580-8025 or 540-665-4509
www.su.edu

These live productions feature professional actors from all over the eastern United States. Matinee and evening performances are offered. Past productions have included *The King and I* and *Steel Magnolias*. Many other musical concerts and performances, from chamber music to jazz, take place in the Ohrstrom-Bryant Theatre year-round.

Shenandoah Valley Music Festival
P.O. Box 528 / Woodstock / 22664
800-459-3396
www.musicfest.org

This relaxed outdoor festival, held in Orkney Springs on the grounds of one of Virginia's oldest mineral springs resorts (the buildings date to Civil War days), has brought music to the mountains for the past four decades. The Fairfax Symphony gives concerts on two weekends in late July. Other concerts from May to September bring Big Band, jazz, bluegrass, and folk music to this scenic, tranquil spot.

Graves Mountain Festival of Music
State Route 670 / Syria / 22743
540-923-4231
www.gravesmountain.com/bluegrass.htm

Graves Mountain Lodge, at the base of the Blue Ridge Mountains near Sperryville, hosts a popular three-day bluegrass concert series on the Thursday, Friday, and Saturday after Memorial Day.

Shenandoah Valley Bach Festival
1200 Park Road / Harrisonburg / 22802
540-432-4582
www.emu.edu/bach

Every June, Eastern Mennonite University sponsors concerts and events highlighting the works of Bach and other composers.

Garth Newel Music Center
P.O. Box 240 / Warm Springs / 24484
877-558-1689 or 540-839-5018
www.garthnewel.org

In addition to classical musical events throughout the year, Garth Newel offers its Summer Chamber Music Festival concerts on Saturday nights and Sunday afternoons. Rooms are available in a 1920s manor house and a 1930s cottage. Weekend dinners are offered in the summer.

Opera Roanoke
541 Luck Avenue / Roanoke / 24016
540-982-2742
www.operaroanoke.org

Since 1977, this company has been performing classics like *Madame Butterfly* as well as modern opera at Shaftman Performance Hall. Five performances are given during the season, which runs from September through May.

Roanoke Symphony Orchestra
541 Luck Avenue / Roanoke / 24016
540-343-6221
www.rso.com

A total of 11 concerts—three chamber music, three pops, and five classical—are given at the new Shaftman Performance Hall and the Roanoke Civic Center. If you'd like to take in the RSO's popular holiday pops concert in early December, buy tickets early. The orchestra also holds concerts in several area towns and cities throughout the year; consult the website for a schedule.

Floyd World Music Festival
Across the Way Productions, 114-B South Locust Street /
**   Floyd / 24091**
540-745-FEST
www.floydfest.com

Held on the last weekend in September, this show spotlights a wide variety of music, from rhythm-and-blues to reggae to bluegrass to Irish and more.

Friday Night Jamboree at Floyd Country Store
South Locust Street / Floyd / 24091
540-745-4563
www.floydcountrystore.com

A jamboree takes place every Friday night in this old country store, which has been described as one of the best places in the country to hear bluegrass music. A Saturday-night concert series features scheduled performers.

Black Dog Jazz Concerts
Château Morrisette Winery
  P.O. Box 766 / Meadows of Dan / 24120
540-593-2865
www.thedogs.com

Outdoor jazz concerts are held monthly from June through October at this mountaintop winery on the Blue Ridge Parkway.

Old Fiddler's Convention
P.O. Box 655 / Galax / 24333
276-236-8541
www.oldfiddlersconvention.com

Bluegrass music lovers from all over have come to Galax each August for nearly 70 years. This six-night affair is the oldest event of its kind in the country. In addition to music, there are arts and crafts and food booths.

Carter Family Fold
P.O. Box 111 / Hiltons / 24258
276-386-9480

Bluegrass and old-time music are performed every Saturday night at the Carter family homeplace in southwestern Virginia near Abingdon. In August, visitors enjoy a weekend music festival that includes food and crafts.

Romantic Getaway

IN AND AROUND
VIRGINIA BEACH AND NORFOLK

Virginia Beach is more than sand, water, and a great new concrete boardwalk—it's the state's largest city, with plenty going on to prove it. Norfolk has become much more cosmopolitan in recent years. It boasts a first-class art museum, lovely old homes and gardens, music and theatrical performances, and good restaurants. The charming little village of Smithfield is nearby, when you're ready to slow down a bit.

THINGS TO DO

- ♥ Rent a bike and ride the three miles of newly widened boardwalk at Virginia Beach, the result of a $100 million makeover
- ♥ Learn about the animals and ecology of the Chesapeake Bay region at the Virginia Marine Science Museum (see pages 154-55); don't miss the 300,000-gallon open-ocean aquarium
- ♥ Enjoy the varied exhibits and collections at the Chrysler Museum of Art (see page 26); don't miss the extensive collection of Tiffany glass
- ♥ Stroll the lush grounds of the Norfolk Botanical Gardens (see page 76)
- ♥ Take a tall-ship cruise on the Elizabeth River (see page 92)
- ♥ Munch on Crackerjacks while watching the minor-league Norfolk Tides (see page 115), a New York Mets farm team that plays in Harbor Park, one of baseball's prettiest stadiums, right on the Norfolk waterfront
- ♥ Nightclub-hop in Norfolk's Ghent neighborhood
- ♥ If you can't make it to Africa this year, do the next best thing and

take in the Okavango Delta exhibit at the Virginia Zoo (see page 72)

♥ Take a riverboat cruise on the *Carrie B* (see page 93) from Norfolk's harbor

♥ Taste Cajun dishes and listen to music at the Bayou Boogaloo and Cajun Food Festival each June (see page 40)

♥ Watch artists at work in their studios at the d'Art Center (see page 30)

♥ Enjoy a play or concert at dramatic Chrysler Hall (see page 9)

♥ In June, attend the Boardwalk Art Show and Festival (see page 45)

♥ From mid-April to mid-May, enjoy the many musical and arts events of the regional Virginia Arts Festival (see page 45)

♥ Experience musical drama at the Harrison Opera House (see page 8)

♥ Groove to a concert at the Verizon Wireless Virginia Beach Amphitheater (see page 9)

♥ Play golf at Heron Ridge or TPC in Virginia Beach, two of the state's top-rated courses (see page 105)

♥ Learn about life at sea at the National Maritime Center, better known as Nauticus (see pages 143-44)

♥ Hike a nature trail or boardwalk at Back Bay National Wildlife Refuge (see pages 61-62)

♥ Sign up for a whale- or dolphin-watching tour at the Virginia Marine Science Museum (see pages 90 and 154-55)

♥ Take a canoe or kayak eco-tour of the area's marshes, creeks, and bays (see pages 89-90)

♥ Visit First Landing State Park (see page 65) to see where the first English settlers arrived in 1607

♥ Cross the famous Chesapeake Bay Bridge/Tunnel to the Eastern Shore to bird-watch or hike at Kiptopeke State Park (see page 64) or to play golf at highly rated Bay Creek in Cape Charles (see page 104)

♥ Head east to the charming little town of Smithfield, where those famous hams are cured; shop and dine on its quaint main street lined with colorful Victorian homes

♥ Pick up a brochure at Smithfield's visitor center and take a self-guided walking tour

♥ For a different kind of tour, hire a horse-drawn carriage (starring Elvis the horse) at Smithfield Horse and Carriage Company (P.O. Box 29 / Smithfield / 23432; 757-635-9963 or 757-357-2035)

PLACES TO EAT

♥ Doumar's Drive-In / Norfolk (see page 164)

♥ Todd Jurich's Bistro / Norfolk (see page 167)

♥ Omar's Carriage House / Norfolk (see pages 167-68)

♥ Alexander's on the Bay / Virginia Beach (see page 168)

♥ Il Giardino Ristorante / Virginia Beach (see pages 168-69)

♥ Lucky Star / 1608 Pleasure House Road / Virginia Beach / 23455; 757-363-8410

♥ Lynnhaven Fish House Restaurant / 2350 Starfish Road / Virginia Beach / 23451; 757-481-0003

♥ The Jewish Mother (deli food) / 3108 Pacific Avenue / Virginia Beach / 23451; 757-422-5430

♥ The Smithfield Inn (see page 207)

PLACES TO STAY

♥ The 11,000 rooms in beachfront hotels and condos in Virginia Beach

♥ The Page House Inn / Norfolk (see page 208)

♥ The Smithfield Inn (see page 207)

♥ Smithfield Station (see page 207)

FOR MORE INFORMATION

♥ Hampton Roads Partnership / 430 World Trade Center / Norfolk / 23510; www.visithamptonroads.com

♥ Virginia Beach Convention and Visitors Bureau / 2100 Parks Avenue / Virginia Beach / 23451; 800-822-3224; www.vbfun.com

♥ Norfolk Convention and Visitors Bureau / 232 East Main Street / Norfolk / 23510; 800-368-3097 or 757-664-6620; www.norfolkcvb.com

♥ Smithfield and Isle of Wight Convention and Visitors Bureau / 130 Main Street / Smithfield / 23431; 800-365-9339; www.smithfield-virginia.org

THEATER

Signature Theater
3806 South Four Mile Run Drive / Arlington / 22206
703-218-6500
www.sig-online.org

The Signature Theater puts on a variety of theatrical performances, including a cabaret and free summer concerts at Lubber Run Amphitheater.

Virginia Stage Company
Monticello Avenue and Tazewell Street, P.O. Box 3770 /
   Norfolk / 23514
757-627-1234
www.vastage.com

Visitors can see Broadway shows performed in historic Wells Theatre, a restored 1912 Beaux-Arts building in downtown Norfolk.

Hampton Roads Shakespeare Festival
Summer Shakes, Inc., 432 24th Street / Virginia Beach /
   23451
757-425-1154
www.summershakes.com

Visitors can enjoy Shakespeare under the stars in the festival's new home at the former Seatack Elementary School in Virginia Beach.

 Shakespeare at the Ruins
Four County Players, Box 1 / Barboursville / 22923
888-427-4427 or 540-832-5355
www.barboursvillewine.com

Over four weekends in July and August, the Four County Players present Shakespeare plays under the stars at the ruins of the Barboursville mansion, located on the grounds of the Barboursville Vineyards (see pages 182-83). The brick house, designed by Thomas Jefferson and built for Governor James Barbour between 1814 and 1822, was destroyed by fire in 1884. The winery offers wine and a buffet dinner before the show. Reservations may be made through the Four County Players.

 The Cultural Arts Center at Glen Allen
2880 Mountain Road, P.O. Box 1249 / Glen Allen / 23060
804-261-6200
www.artsglenallen.com

A range of arts—theater, dance, music, and fine art—are celebrated in this recently restored schoolhouse near Richmond.

Barksdale Theatre
1601 Willow Lawn Drive / Richmond / 23230
804-282-2620
www.barksdalerichmond.org

The longest-running live theater in Richmond, Barksdale offers contemporary dramatic and musical productions year-round.

Encore Theatre Company
P.O. Box 27543 / Richmond / 23261
888-DRAMA-88
www.richmondshakespeare.com

The Encore Theatre Company sponsors the Richmond Shakespeare Festival, which takes place on the lawn at Agecroft Hall, an old English home moved from across the Atlantic in the 1920s. It also performs at the Fulton School Studios.

Theatre Virginia
2800 Grove Avenue / Richmond / 23221
877-353-6161 or
804-353-6161
www.theatreva.com

This not-for-profit professional theater is located in the Virginia Museum of Fine Arts. Its season, which features dramas and comedies, runs from October through June.

Wayside Theatre
7853 Main Street, US 11, P.O. Box 260 / Middletown /
22645
800-951-1776 or 540-869-1776
www.waysidetheatre.org

Wayside Theatre has been a tradition for nearly 40 years.

Professional actors perform classic and contemporary dramas in matinee and evening performances May through October and in December.

 Court Square Theater
61 Graham Street, P.O. Box 1051 /
Harrisonburg / 22803
540-433-9189
www.courtsquaretheater.com

This nonprofit theater, located in a modern facility across the street from the county courthouse, is operated by the Arts Council of the Valley. It features a wide variety of performances in dance, music (from classical to bluegrass), theater, and film.

 Shenandoah Shakespeare's
Blackfriars Playhouse
11 East Beverley Street /
Staunton / 24401
540-885-4886
www.ishakespeare.com

Visitors can see authentic Shakespeare dramas performed year-round by the Shenandoah Shakespeare Company in its new 300-seat facility, the Blackfriars Playhouse, which was modeled after the original Blackfriars Theatre in London.

highlight

Virginia's Historic Drive-In Movie Theaters: Still Playing

If you're of a certain age, you can relive your youth by watching movies with your love under the stars at one of the handful of drive-in theaters left in Virginia. Interestingly, all but one are on historic US 11. Two are in the Shenandoah Valley: Hull's Drive-In Theatre, north of Lexington (540-643-2621 / www.hullsdrivein.com), and the Family Drive-In Theatre, between Strasburg and Winchester in Stephens City (540-869-2175). The rest are in southwestern Virginia: the Moonlite Theatre in Abingdon (276-628-7881), the Hiland Drive-In in Rural Retreat, south of Wytheville (276-686-5661), the Park Place Drive-In and Fun Center in Marion (276-781-2222), and the Starlite Drive-In in Christiansburg (540-382-2202). The only Virginia drive-in not on US 11 is the Central Drive-In in Norton (276-679-3761). At one time or another, nearly 200 drive-in theaters operated in the state.

Theater at Lime Kiln
P.O. Box 663 / Lexington / 24450
540-463-3074
www.theateratlimekiln.com

Plays and concerts are offered at two outdoor theaters week-nights and weekends from May through September in this scenic spot outside Lexington. Past musical performers have included Janis Ian and Robin and Linda Williams. Lawn seating is available, and visitors are welcome to bring a picnic.

Mill Mountain Theatre
Center in the Square / Roanoke / 24011
540-342-5740
www.millmountain.org

Professional theatrical productions are offered on two stages throughout the year at this theater in downtown Roanoke.

Barter Theatre
133 West Main Street / Abingdon / 24210
276-628-3991
www.bartertheatre.com

The Barter Theatre is the state theater of Virginia. Its name dates back to the theater's beginnings in 1933, when canned goods and other food items could be used to gain admission; cash or credit cards are preferred today. Broadway shows and musicals are performed here year-round.

Romantic Getaway

ROANOKE

Roanoke sits in a valley of its own—the Roanoke Valley—at the southern end of the Shenandoah Valley, not far off the Blue Ridge Parkway and I-81. It's one of the state's "newer" cities, historically speaking. It grew from a small town called Big Lick into a booming railroad hub practically overnight beginning in the 1880s. Roanoke remains a growing, vibrant city with much to offer in the way of cultural events and outdoor activities.

THINGS TO DO

- ♥ Shop the 60 yellow-and-white-awninged stalls at the historic Roanoke City Farmers' Market (open daily except Sunday), as well as the food and wine shops in the market area
- ♥ Next door at the Center in the Square, visit the art (see pages 28-29), science (see page 156), and history (see pages 150-51) museums
- ♥ Experience a performance of Opera Roanoke (see page 12)
- ♥ Enjoy live classical music performed by the Roanoke Symphony Orchestra (see page 13)
- ♥ Learn about the romantic days of railroading at the Virginia Museum of Transportation (see page 150)
- ♥ Visit the historic town of Salem, just south of Roanoke
- ♥ Watch the Salem Avalanche play minor-league baseball (see page 116)
- ♥ Enjoy the nearby Mill Mountain Zoo (see pages 72-73) or Virginia's Explore Park (see page 63), where you can ride a batteau or rent a bike or canoe

♥ In Blacksburg, cheer for the Virginia Tech Hokies at a Big East football game (see page 119)

♥ Experience the excitement of professional ice hockey at a game of the Roanoke Express (see page 119)

♥ Head northwest to stroll the quiet streets of Fincastle, an 1800s gateway to the West that remains well preserved and off the beaten path today

♥ Play golf at the highly rated River Course in Radford (see page 106)

♥ Drive the Blue Ridge Parkway south to sample Italian-style wines in a recreated Tuscan farmhouse at Villa Appalaccia Winery (see pages 186-87)

♥ A little farther south on the parkway, take romantic pictures of historic Mabry Mill (see page 145), located at Milepost 176 near the Meadows of Dan

♥ Venture a short way south and west off the Blue Ridge Parkway to enjoy country and bluegrass music or to visit the antique shops in the town of Floyd; if you're there on a weekend night, don't miss the fun and live music at the legendary Floyd Country Store (see page 13), considered one of the best places in the country to hear bluegrass

♥ Stretch out on the lawn at the Meadows of Dan and groove to live jazz on the second Saturday in June, July, and August at the Château Morrisette Winery (see page 185)

♥ In Dublin, 50 miles south of Roanoke, hike, camp, bike, and swim at Claytor Lake State Park (see page 68)

♥ In Bedford, visit the National D-Day Memorial (see pages 147)

♥ In Forest, east of Bedford and south of Lynchburg, tour Thomas Jefferson's octagonal summer retreat, Poplar Forest (see page 136)

PLACES TO EAT

- ♥ The Regency Dining Room in the Hotel Roanoke (see page 175)
- ♥ Carlos Brazilian International Cuisine / Roanoke (see page 174)
- ♥ Wertz's Restaurant and Wine Bar / 215 Market Street / Roanoke / 24011; 540-342-5133
- ♥ Billy's Ritz / 102 Salem Avenue / Roanoke / 24011; 540-342-3937
- ♥ Oddfellas Cantina / Floyd (see page 175)
- ♥ Pine Tavern / 611 Floyd Highway North / Floyd / 24091; 540-745-4482

PLACES TO STAY

- ♥ The Hotel Roanoke (see page 220)
- ♥ Nesselrod on the New Gardens and Guesthouse / Radford (see pages 220-21)
- ♥ The Inn at Burwell Place / 601 West Main Street / Salem / 24153; 540-387-0250
- ♥ CrossTrails Bed and Breakfast (crossroads of the Appalachian Trail and the Trans-America Bicycle Trail) / 5880 Blacksburg Road / Catawba / 24070; 800-841-8078 or 540-384-8078
- ♥ Stonewall Bed and Breakfast / Floyd (see page 221)

FOR MORE INFORMATION

- ♥ Roanoke Valley Convention and Visitors Bureau / 114 Market Street / Roanoke / 24011; 800-635-5535; www.visitroanokeva.com

DANCE

Virginia Ballet Theatre
134 West Olney Road / Norfolk / 23510
757-622-4822
www.chm.net/ballet/default.htm

Richmond Ballet
407 East Canal Street / Richmond / 23219
804-344-0906
www.richmondballet.com

ART MUSEUMS

Chrysler Museum of Art
245 West Olney Road / Norfolk / 23510
757-664-6200
www.chrysler.org

This jewel of a museum has something for everyone. Roman, Greek, and Egyptian artifacts, an outstanding Tiffany glass collection (as well as many other types of glass), decorative arts, and five centuries' worth of European (Italian, Dutch, Flemish, French, British, Spanish) and American paintings and sculpture form the core of the collection. Among the notable holdings are works by Rubens, Gauguin, Degas, Renoir, Cezanne, Matisse, and Cassatt. Twentieth-century American art, including works by Calder, Lichtenstein, and Rothko, are also in the museum's permanent collection. Two nearby historic homes—the Moses Myers House and the Willoughby-Baylor House—are part of the museum.

Belmont, the Gari Melchers Estate and Memorial Gallery
224 Washington Street /
    Fredericksburg / 22405
540-654-1015
http://departments.mwc.edu/
    belm/www

Located outside Fredericksburg, Belmont was once the home of Gari Melchers, an American artist who died in 1932. Visitors can tour the lovely old home, its extensive gardens (restored by the Garden Club of Virginia), and the artist's stone studio, which serves as a gallery for many of his works. Weddings may be held in the gardens.

University of Virginia Art Museum
Thomas H. Bayly Building, 155
    Rugby Road, P.O. Box 400119 /
    Charlottesville / 22904
434-924-3592
www.virginia.edu/artmuseum

This museum features some 9,000 objects, including American and European paintings; Asian, African, and Native American art; and art from the ancient Mediterranean.

---

highlight

Art Museums in Colonial Williamsburg

Art lovers will enjoy touring two special museums in Colonial Williamsburg. The DeWitt Wallace Decorative Arts Museum, at Francis and North Henry Streets, showcases English and American antique furniture, ceramics, textiles, clothing, and other objects dating to the 17th century. The Lila Acheson Wallace Garden, located on the grounds of the museum, is unique—for Williamsburg, anyway—in that it is a delightful modern garden, not an 18th-century re-creation. Call 757-220-7724 for information. The Abby Aldrich Rockefeller Folk Art Museum, on South England Street across from the Williamsburg Lodge, contains collections of all kinds of folk art from colonial times, including paintings, toys, and needlework. Both museums charge admission. For more information on hours, events, and exhibits, call 800-HISTORY or 757-220-7690 or visit www.colonialwilliamsburg.com.

Kluge-Ruhe Aboriginal Art Collection
University of Virginia, 400 Peter Jefferson Place /
    Charlottesville / 22911
434-244-0234
www.virginia.edu/kluge-ruhe

Located on the outskirts of Charlottesville, this intriguing, relatively new museum (established in 1997) holds one of the world's largest collections of Australian art.

Virginia Museum of Fine Arts
2800 Grove Avenue / Richmond / 23221
804-340-1400
www.vmfa.state.va.us

The state's premier art museum offers collections from around the world, including ancient Greek, Roman, and Egyptian treasures; medieval and Renaissance art; objects from Africa, China, Japan, and India; a superb collection of Art Nouveau and Art Deco works; French impressionist and British sporting art; and the Pratt Collection of jeweled Fabergé objects.

Maier Museum of Art
Randolph-Macon Woman's College, 2500 Rivermont Avenue /
    Lynchburg / 24503
434-947-8136
www.rmwc.edu/maier

The Maier showcases American art, including works by Whistler, Homer, Cassatt, O'Keeffe, Benton, Hopper, and Wyeth.

Art Museum of Western Virginia
Center in the Square, 1 Market Square / Roanoke / 24011
540-342-5760
www.artmuseumroanoke.org

Featured in this popular and growing art museum are 19th- and 20th-century American paintings, photos, and sculpture.

 William King Regional Arts Center
415 Academy Drive, P.O. Box 2256 / Abingdon / 24212
276-628-5005
www.wkrac.org

The center, an affiliate of the Virginia Museum of Fine Arts, features changing exhibits of sculpture, photography, and paintings.

ART GALLERIES

There are dozens of quality art and crafts galleries all over the state. A few of the largest and best known are described below. For a comprehensive list, visit the website of the Virginia Commission for the Arts at www.arts.state.va.us, which gives information on retail galleries by region, plus links to numerous Virginia artists and art organizations. For a list of select arts and crafts festivals and shows, see pages 44-46.

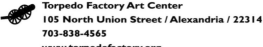 **Torpedo Factory Art Center**
105 North Union Street / Alexandria / 22314
703-838-4565
www.torpedofactory.org

Visitors can browse the works of more than 160 diverse artists and watch as they create sculpture, paintings, stained glass, jewelry, ceramics, and more. The center is located alongside the Potomac River in a renovated weapons factory.

The Peninsula Fine Arts Center
101 Museum Drive / Newport News / 23606
757-596-8175
www.pfac-va.org

Located across the street from the Mariners' Museum, this gallery offers exhibits of sculpture, paintings, and photographs by regional artists, plus an art school and educational programs.

d'Art Center
125 College Place / Norfolk / 23510
757-625-4211

More than 30 professional artists work in open studios in this renovated downtown building, where visitors can watch their creations in progress. Classes and exhibits are also offered.

Contemporary Art Center of Virginia
2200 Parks Avenue / Virginia Beach / 23451
757-425-0000
www.cacv.org

The Contemporary Art Center of Virginia offers changing exhibits and sponsors the Boardwalk Art Show and the Neptune Festival, two top-rated outdoor fine-arts shows.

Second Street Gallery
201 Second Street NW / Charlottesville / 22902
434-977-7284
www.monticello.avenue.org/ssg

This gallery, founded in 1973 and located on the first floor of the McGuffey Art Center a block off the downtown mall, showcases alternative contemporary art.

Shockoe Bottom Arts Center
2001 East Grace Street / Richmond / 23223
804-643-7959
www.shockoebottomarts.com

The center displays the works of more than 200 artists, many of whom have studios here.

Artspace
6 East Broad Street / Richmond / 23219
804-782-8672
www.artspacegallery.org

This nonprofit gallery in downtown Richmond displays the works of area contemporary artists.

Artisans Center of Virginia
601 Shenandoah Village Drive / Waynesboro / 22980
877-508-6069 or 540-946-3294
www.artisansva.com

This is the state's official artisans' center. It features juried crafts from more than 130 professional Virginia craftspeople.

Shenandoah Valley Art Center
600 West Main Street / Waynesboro / 22980
540-949-7662
www.artsvirginia.com/SVAC.htm

Works of local artists are displayed in this lovely old home in downtown Waynesboro.

Artists in Cahoots
1 West Washington Street / Lexington / 24450
540-464-1147
www.artistsincahoots.com

For more than 20 years, this member-run gallery has occupied the ground floor of one of Lexington's historic downtown buildings.

The Arts Depot
314 Depot Square / Abingdon / 24212
276-628-9091
www.abingdonartsdepot.org

Resident artists have studios in the gallery. They specialize in painting, fiber arts, weaving, pottery, sculpture, and jewelry. Many other local artists' works are displayed as well.

Romantic Getaway

RICHMOND

Richmond is jam-packed with Virginia history, from before the Revolution to the Civil War and after. It's a fun, compact, easy-to-see city with good restaurants, fine lodging, distinctive old neighborhoods, and varied cultural attractions.

THINGS TO DO

- Visit the 1788 State Capitol Building (see page 135), designed by Thomas Jefferson, and its grounds; inside, admire the only true-to-life statue of George Washington ever made
- Take a stroll along the Canal Walk on the James River downtown (or ride a boat or barge)
- Thrill to an urban whitewater raft ride on Richmond's downtown rapids, courtesy of the Richmond Raft Company (see page 91)

- Shop and enjoy lunch or the nightlife at one of the many establishments in historic Shockoe Slip and Shockoe Bottom along the James River
- While in Shockoe Bottom, honor a famous writer who lived in Richmond for many years by visiting the Edgar Allen Poe Museum (see page 146)
- Take a 10-mile lunch cruise on the James aboard the *Annabel Lee* riverboat (see page 93)
- Attend a performance of the Virginia Ballet (see page 26) or the Richmond Symphony Orchestra (see page 10)
- Tour the collections and the sculpture garden at the Virginia Museum of Fine Arts (see page 28)
- Visit Richmond's other museums, including the Science Museum of Virginia with its IMAX Dome and Planetarium (see page 156), and the Museum of the Confederacy (see page 146)
- Spend a morning or an afternoon visiting the several attractions at Maymont (see pages 77-78)—its Italian and Japanese gardens, its turn-of-the-century mansion house, and its new nature center overlooking the James River
- Take a long walk at the Lewis Ginter Botanical Garden (see page 77); break for a cup of tea in its Japanese tea garden
- Visit the park-like grounds of Hollywood Cemetery, a favorite haunt of Richmond insiders; enjoy great views of the James River and see the tombs of United States presidents Monroe and Tyler
- Walk or drive around the Fan District, the largest intact Victorian community in the United States, located between Boulevard and Belvedere Streets and Main and Broad Streets
- Explore Carytown, a lively city neighborhood with many fun shops and eateries; pick up a robust cup of coffee at Rostov's at 2902 Cary Street and head across the street for a sinful treat at For the Love of Chocolate
- Treat yourself to the fabulous Sunday brunch in the Palm Court of the historic Jefferson Hotel (see page 213)

PLACES TO EAT

- ♥ Amici Ristorante (see page 171)
- ♥ Lemaire at the Jefferson Hotel (see pages 171-72)
- ♥ Zeus Gallery (see page 172)
- ♥ The Dining Room at the Berkeley Hotel (see page 172)

PLACES TO STAY

- ♥ The Jefferson Hotel (see page 212)
- ♥ The Berkeley Hotel (see page 214)
- ♥ Linden Row Inn (see pages 213-14)

FOR MORE INFORMATION

- ♥ Richmond Metropolitan Convention and Visitors Bureau / 405 North Third Street / 23219; 888-RICHMOND or 804-358-5511; www.richmondva.org

Fairs
and
Festivals

A heart that overflows may seek out merrymaking and boisterous festivities to quietly rejoice, unnoticed amidst the reveling crowds.
Franz Grillparzer, 19th-century Austrian author

Virginia is a fair- and festival-loving state, with hundreds taking place throughout the year celebrating everything from goats to garlic. I've arranged a selection of the most popular fests into three categories: Food and Wine, Arts and Crafts, and Everything Under the Sun. A sampling of the state's many music festivals is included in the section that starts on page 6. And although they're not listed here—there are just so many—don't forget about the many town, city, and county fairs and fests held all over the state. For a monthly calendar of all Virginia festivals, visit www.southfest.com or do a search of Virginia by month at www.festivalnet.com.

FOOD AND WINE

More than 300 wine-related events take place throughout the year at the 80 Virginia wineries and other locations. For a complete listing by month, visit www.virginiawines.org. At this site, you can also order the free, annual *Virginia Wineries Festival and Tour Guide*, which describes all the wineries and includes a calendar of events.

Virginians love any excuse to sample their favorite foods, from Chesapeake Bay oysters and clams in the fall to maple doughnuts in Highland County in early spring. A few of the more notable fests are listed below. For a complete listing of Virginia food festivals, check out www.vdacs.state.va.us/news/festival.html.

One event of note that's not in Virginia is the Washington, D.C., International Wine Festival, held in early March. It brings in more than 200 wineries from around the world and features seminars, cooking demonstrations, and a Sunday brunch. Call 800-343-1174 for details, or visit www.wine-expos.com.

Mount Vernon Wine Tasting Festival and Sunset Tour
P.O. Box 110 / Mount Vernon / 22121
703-780-2000
www.mountvernon.org

Held on the grounds of Mount Vernon, this annual event takes place on three weekend nights in May. It offers wine tastings, live jazz, and tours of the cellars where President Washington stored his wine. This event sells out quickly; tickets go on sale April 1.

Vintage Virginia Wine Festival
P.O. Box 3182 / Annapolis, MD / 21403
800-277-CORK
www.vintagevirginia.com

Many of the state's wineries are represented at this large annual festival held in early June. It takes place at Great Meadows in The Plains. Great Meadows is off I-66 east of Front Royal.

Virginia Wine Festival
800-520-9670
www.showsinc.com/vawf

The state's oldest and largest wine festival is held every August at Great Meadows in The Plains. More than 40 wineries offer tastings. Visitors also enjoy music, food, and arts and crafts.

Graves Mountain Apple Harvest Festival
Graves Mountain Lodge / Syria / 22743
540-923-4231
www.gravesmountain.com

Syria is south of Sperryville in the foothills of the Blue Ridge Mountains, a perfect setting for a festival celebrating bluegrass music, arts and crafts, food cooked over an open fire, and more. You can even pick your own apples in the Graves Mountain orchards.

Eastern Shore Seafood Festival
Eastern Shore of Virginia Chamber of Commerce,
**   P.O. Drawer 460 / Melfa / 23410**
757-787-2460
www.esvachamber.org

All-you-can-eat seafood and free entertainment are the main draws at this celebration, held in May at Tom's Cove Campground on Chincoteague Island.

Chincoteague Oyster Festival
Chincoteague Chamber of Commerce, P.O. Box 258 /
  Chincoteague Island / 23336
757-336-6161
www.chincoteaguechamber.com

Oysters, clams fritters, hush puppies, and more serve to welcome the oyster season each October.

Urbanna Oyster Festival
Drawer C / Urbanna / 23175
www.urbanna.com

Held in early November, this annual fest celebrates oyster season with craft booths, art exhibits, and food stands offering oysters served every which way: raw, roasted, steamed, stewed, fried, and frittered. It's also fun to watch shuckers compete at the Virginia State Oyster Shucking Championship.

Bayou Boogaloo and Cajun Food Festival
Norfolk Festevents, Ltd , 120 West Main Street / Norfolk /
  23501
757-441-2345
www.festeventsva.org

Town Point Park on the waterfront fills with the sounds and tastes of New Orleans at this popular festival held over three days in June. There are Cajun and Creole cooking demonstrations, concerts, shows, hot pepper eating contests, and plenty of crawfish, about 10,000 pounds of which are served each year.

Neptune Festival Wine Tasting
265 Kings Grant Road, Suite 102 / Virginia Beach / 23452
757-498-0215
www.neptunefestival.com

This beach event takes place in September at the 24th Street Park. Visitors can sample the wares from several Virginia wineries and restaurants. The number of tickets is limited, so order early.

Suffolk Peanut Fest
P.O. Box 1852 / Suffolk / 23439
757-539-6751
www.suffolkfest.org

Over four days in mid-October, the town of Suffolk honors its treasured crop, the peanut, with a parade, arts and crafts exhibits, live music, food stands, a demolition derby, and tractor pulls.

Ash Lawn-Highland Wine Festival
1000 James Monroe Parkway, State Route 795 /
Charlottesville / 22902
434-293-9539
www.avenue.org/ashlawn

James Monroe's home near Monticello outside Charlottesville is the setting for this popular May wine festival, which features music, food, and house tours.

Montpelier Wine Festival
11407 Constitution Highway, State Route 20 / Montpelier
Station / 22957
540-672-0014
www.montpelier.org

Held yearly in early May on the grounds of James Madison's home in Orange County, this fest features wines from area wineries, hot-air balloon rides, food, crafts, and kite-flying exhibitions.

Herbs Galore
Maymont Foundation, 1700 Hampton Street / Richmond /
    23220
804-358-7166
www.maymont.org

Held on the lush and lovely grounds of Maymont, this fest features plant sales, seminars, live music, and food.

Virginia Wine and Garlic Festival
Rebec Vineyards, 221 North Amherst Highway / Amherst /
    24521
804-946-5168
www.rebecwinery.com

Rebec Vineyards, north of Lynchburg, sponsors this garlic lovers' event each October. Visitors enjoy wine tastings from several area wineries, music, crafts, and a garlic cookoff.

Virginia Cantaloupe Festival
Halifax County Chamber of Commerce, P.O. Box 399 /
    South Boston / 24592
888-458-1003 or 434-572-3085
www.valopefest.com

The highlight at this fun fair at the Halifax County Fairgrounds is all-you-can-eat cantaloupe. You can also get Brunswick stew and corn on the cob.

Virginia Wine and Mushroom Festival
414 East Main Street / Front Royal / 22630
800-338-2576 or 540-635-3185
www.wineandmushroom.com

More than a dozen wineries and several mushroom vendors are the draw here, along with live entertainment and arts and crafts booths. The festival is held in the Front Royal Historic District every May.

 Highland Maple Festival
Highland County Chamber of Commerce, P.O. Box 223 /
Monterey / 24465
540-468-2250
www.highlandcounty.org

Held during the second and third weekends in March, this festival celebrates maple-syrup making. Since 1958, this has been an annual event in Highland County, located over the mountains west of Staunton.

The Homestead's Annual Food and Wine Spectacular
Homestead Resort, US 220, Main Street, P.O. Box 2000 /
Hot Springs / 24445
800-838-1766 or 540-839-1766
www.thehomestead.com

The famous hot-springs resort offers an April weekend of food and wine tastings and cooking demonstrations. Wineries from Virginia and elsewhere are invited to participate.

Annual Rockbridge Food and Wine Festival at the
Theater at Lime Kiln
Lexington-Rockbridge County Chamber of Commerce,
100 East Washington Street / Lexington / 24450
540-463-5375
www.lexrockchamber.com

This September event, sponsored by the Lexington-Rockbridge County Chamber of Commerce, features food and wine samplings, live music, seminars, and exotic cars.

Roanoke Valley Wine Festival
Roanoke Jaycees, P.O. Box 1225 / Roanoke / 24006
540-345-1316
www.roanokejaycees.com

This event, sponsored by the Roanoke Jaycees, takes place in Explore Park, located just off the Blue Ridge Parkway north of Roanoke. Held in June in conjunction with the Blue Ridge Garden Festival, it offers live music, food, and wine tastings.

ARTS AND CRAFTS

Waterford Homes Tour and Crafts Exhibit
Waterford Foundation, Inc., P.O. Box 142 / Waterford /
20197
540-882-3018
www.waterfordva.org

This National Historic Landmark Village is home to the oldest juried crafts fair in the state. Be prepared to join the crowds that descend on this tiny town each October to view the works of hundreds of quality craftspeople.

Northern Virginia Fine Arts Festival
11911 Freedom Drive, Suite 110 / Reston / 20190
703-471-9242

Each May, nearly 200 painters, sculptors, and craftspeople participate in this juried show at the Greater Reston Arts Center.

Historic Occoquan Arts and Crafts Show
Occoquan Town Hall, 314 Mill Street, P.O. Box 195 /
   Occoquan / 22125
703-491-2168

Occoquan is a historic Potomac waterfront town south of Alexandria near I-95. It hosts this popular show twice a year, in the spring and fall. More than 300 exhibitors participate.

Virginia Arts Festival
220 Boush Street / Norfolk / 23510
757-282-2800
www.vaintlartsfest.com

This popular festival, held since 1997, runs from mid-April to mid-May. It celebrates arts of all kinds—visual arts, dance, popular and classical music, and theater. In all, about 90 performances are given. The events are held in a variety of venues in eight cities in the Virginia Beach/Norfolk area.

Boardwalk Art Show
Contemporary Art Center of Virginia, 2200 Parks Avenue /
   Virginia Beach / 23451
757-425-0000
www.cacv.org/bw.html

Each June, more than 300 artists and craftspeople participate in this juried, nationally ranked, four-day show on 14 blocks of boardwalk.

Crozet Arts and Crafts Festival
Claudius Crozet Park, P.O. Box 171 / Crozet / 22932
434-823-2211
http://avenue.org/ccp/artcraft.htm

This juried show features the work of more than 100 artists and craftspeople. It is held at Claudius Crozet Park twice a year—on Mother's Day weekend and the second weekend in October. Crozet is a little village in the mountains near Charlottesville.

Everything Under the Sun

Oatlands Sheep Dog Trials
28050 Oatlands Plantation Lane / Leesburg / 20175
703-777-3174

Usually held the second weekend in May, this unusual event features border collies and their handlers demonstrating herding work in the fields. Crafts, food, and music round out the attractions.

Potomac Celtic Festival
Morven Park Equestrian Center, State Route 15 and
  Tutt Lane / Leesburg
800-752-6118
www.PotomacCelticFest.org

Visitors to this top-rated festival can listen to live Celtic music on eight stages, shop for arts and crafts, see living-history demonstrations, watch Scottish games, sample ethnic foods, and do much more. Held the second weekend in June, the festival celebrates the Celtic culture of Cornwall, Ireland, Scotland, Wales, the Isle of Man, Galicia, Asturias, and Brittany.

August Court Days
Loudon Restoration and Preservation Society, P.O. Box 351 /
Leesburg / 20175
800-752-6118

More than 200 costumed living-history interpreters reenact life in colonial Virginia. Visitors can enjoy militia drills, mock trials, folk and country music concerts, dancers, strolling entertainers, and crafts.

Hunt Country Stable Tour
Trinity Episcopal Church, P.O. Box 127 / Upperville / 20185
540-592-3711
www.middleburgonline.com/stabletour

This event allows visitors to take a self-guided driving tour of thoroughbred breeding farms and country estates in and around Middleburg, Upperville, and The Plains. A catered lunch at one of four historic buildings along US 50 is part of the festival, held over two days in late May.

Celebrate Fairfax
12000 Government Center Parkway, Suite 565 / Fairfax /
22035
800-880-6629 or 703-324-FAIR
www.celebratefairfax.com

Formerly known as the Fairfax Festival, this event is held each June at the County Government Center off I-66. It draws up to 100,000 visitors and more than 300 exhibitors, vendors, and craftspeople. Big-name musical entertainers perform on seven stages, and there's food, hot-air balloon rides, and nightly fireworks.

Manassas Heritage Railway Festival
Historic Manassas, Inc., 9431 West Street / Manassas / 20110
703-361-6599
www.visitmanassas.org

Those who come to this event in Old Town Manassas in early June can ride the rails, listen to live music, and view exhibits focusing on railroad history.

 Grand Illumination
Colonial Williamsburg Foundation, P.O. Box 1776 /
**   Williamsburg / 23187**
800-HISTORY
www.colonialwilliamsburg.org

Colonial Williamsburg welcomes the holiday season in early December with a celebration that lights up the historic area with candles. Visitors also enjoy fireworks, music, dancing, caroling, and dramatic presentations on multiple stages throughout the historic area.

 International Azalea Festival
220 Boush Street, P.O. Box 3595 / Norfolk / 23514
757-282-2801
www.azaleafestival.org

This fest has an interesting mission: To celebrate spring and to offer appreciation to the North Atlantic Treaty Organization (NATO). There's a parade of nations, a performance by the group known as the Virginia International Tattoo, art exhibits, an air show, and the Azalea Queen's coronation.

Norfolk Harborfest
Norfolk Festevents, Ltd., 120 West Main Street / Norfolk /
    23501
757-441-2345
www.festeventsva.org

Held in various locations in town, this festival salutes ships
and boats of all kinds—tall ships, military vessels, tugboats, and
Chesapeake Bay workboats. It also features live entertainment,
food, and fireworks.

 Neptune Festival
265 Kings Grant Road, Suite 102 / Virginia Beach / 23452
866-NEP-FEST or 757-498-0215
www.neptunefestival.com

Every September, visitors to Virginia Beach celebrate the
end of summer at one of the oldest and best seaside fests in the
South. The Boardwalk Weekend features a sand-sculpting contest, fireworks, and arts and crafts.

 100 Miles of Lights
Newport News Visitor Center, 13560 Jefferson Avenue /
    Newport News / 23603
888-493-7386, ext. 100
www.newport-news.org/groupinfo/100milesoflights.htm

From around Thanksgiving until New Year's, the area from
Richmond to Virginia Beach is aglow with drive- and walk-
through light shows, lighted boat parades, and city illumi-
nations. Towns throughout the region put on festivals, parades, musical and dance performances, and living-history
reenactments.

Virginia Festival of the Book
Virginia Foundation for the Humanities, 145 Ednam Drive /
**   Charlottesville / 22903**
434-924-6890 or 434-924-3296
www.vabook.org

This festival takes place at various venues all over Charlottesville during five days in late March. It features author readings and more than 200 book-related programs.

Fall Fiber Festival and Sheep Dog Trials
State Route 20 South / Montpelier Station / 22957
540-672-2935

Held every October at Montpelier, the home of President James Monroe, this fair features sheepdog trials, as well as fiber artists and their fiber sources: sheep, llamas, angora and cashmere goats, and angora rabbits.

State Fair of Virginia
P.O. Box 26805 / Richmond / 23261
800-588-3247 or 804-228-3200
www.statefair.com

The State Fair of Virginia takes place at the Richmond Raceway complex over 11 days in late September and early October. Concerts, food, antiques, racing pigs, livestock shows, a rodeo, carnival rides, historical reenactments, and a demolition derby are just a few of the many events and activities.

James River Batteau Festival
Virginia Canals and Navigation Society, Inc.,
**   6826 Rosemount Drive / McLean / 22101 (mailing address)**
www.batteau.org

Each June, more than a dozen batteaux—the flat-bottomed boats of the 1700s and 1800s—participate in this week-long festival, which takes place along the 120-mile stretch of the James River between Lynchburg and Richmond. These boats were once the primary means of shipping and transportation on the James and other Virginia rivers.

 Virginia Lake Festival
Clarksville Lake Country Chamber of Commerce, 105
    Second Street, P.O. Box 1017 / Clarksville / 23927
800-557-5582 or 434-374-2436
www.kerrlake.com/chamber

Located on the Virginia-North Carolina line, John Kerr Lake (a.k.a. Buggs Island Lake) is the state's largest lake. Held on the third weekend in July, the Virginia Lake Festival features food stands, live entertainment (including clowns, dancers, gymnasts, and musicians), water-skiing demonstrations, hot-air balloon rides, and helicopter rides.

 Shenandoah Apple Blossom Festival
135 North Cameron Street / Winchester / 22601
800-230-2139 or 540-662-3863
www.sabf.org

This classic Virginia festival, held at various venues around town in early May, features more than 30 events, including dances, parades, band competitions, a circus, and celebrity appearances.

 ArborFest
State Arboretum of Virginia, 400 Blandy Farm Lane /
    Boyce / 22620
540-837-1758
www.virginia.edu/~blandy

This event is held the second Sunday in October at Blandy Experimental Farm, located on US 50 nine miles east of Winchester. Visitors can tour the gardens and enjoy music, lectures, and other activities.

Shenandoah Valley Hot Air Balloon and Wine Festival
US 50 / Millwood / 22646
800-662-1360 or 540-837-1856
www.historiclongbranch.com/balloonfest

Historic Long Branch, a beautifully restored 1811 Greek Revival mansion (see page 137), is the site of a festival of hot-air balloons during the third full weekend in October. Visitors can even go for a ride. Millwood is about halfway between Winchester and Front Royal.

Jousting Tournaments
Natural Chimneys Regional Park, 94 Natural Chimneys
Lane / Mount Solon / 22843
540-350-2510
http://home.rica.net/uvrpa/contents.htm

The Hall of Fame Joust takes place here every June. The Natural Chimneys Joust is held on the third Saturday in August, just as it has been since 1821. The castle-like Natural Chimneys offer the perfect backdrop for these Middle Ages-style events.

Chester Farms Wool Fair
3581 Churchville Avenue / Churchville / 24421
877-ONE-WOOL or 540-337-7282
www.chesterfarms.com

Where else can you see sheep being sheared, then watch the process of making wool (hand carding, natural dyeing, and spinning)? The annual wool fair at this farm west of Staunton offers demonstrations throughout the day. Other activities include an arts and crafts show, horse and pony rides, horse-drawn wagon rides, and hayrides.

Dickens of a Christmas
Downtown Roanoke, Inc., 213 Market Street SW / Roanoke / 24011
540-342-2028
www.downtownroanoke.org

Held in early December, this festival re-creates a Victorian-era Christmas, with a parade, a Christmas tree lighting, costumed strolling performers, period entertainment, horse-drawn carriage rides, carolers, and craftspeople. Downtown merchants hand out roasted chestnuts, hot cocoa, and hot apple cider.

Blue Ridge Folklife Festival
Blue Ridge Institute and Museum, Ferrum College,
P.O. Box 1000 / Ferrum / 24088
540-365-4416
www.blueridgeinstitute.org

Highly rated by the *New York Times* and the Southeast Tourism Society, this authentic old-time folk festival offers three stages of music, regional foods, traditional crafts demonstrations, and working animal competitions, including the Virginia State Championship Coon Mule Jumping Contest and the Virginia State Championship Coon Dog Water Race. It's held on the fourth Saturday in October. Ferrum is about 45 minutes south of Roanoke.

Virginia Highlands Festival
P.O. Box 801 / Abingdon / 24212
276-623-5266
www.vahighlandsfestival.org

This big event is held over two weeks in late July and early August. Visitors come to enjoy crafts, antiques, fine arts, and performing arts.

*The
Great
Outdoors*

Far from the bustle of the world, they [the people of the Blue Ridge] are everywhere surrounded with beautiful prospects and sylvan scenes; lofty mountains, transparent streams, falls of water, rich valleys, and majestic woods.

Andrew Barnaby,
English visitor to Virginia, 1760

A walk down a wooded path or along a beach, a mountain hike, a dip in a lake or a waterfall pool, a picnic in the woods—encounters with nature can revive the spirit and rekindle romance. Virginia is arguably one of America's most scenic states, offering outdoor activities for couples of all ages and interests. There's mountain biking, kayaking, skydiving, hot-air ballooning, and mountain climbing for the adventurous, and garden strolls, country drives, bird-watching, and boat cruises for the rest of us. Something beautiful is waiting for you and your love down a Virginia road or highway.

NATIONAL PARKS, FORESTS, AND SEASHORES

For detailed information about national parks and forests

in the state, go to www.recreation.gov and type Virginia in the search box.

 Assateague Island National Seashore
7206 National Seashore Lane, P.O. Box 38 / Berlin, MD /
    21811
    410-641-1441

The southern entrance to this 37-mile-long barrier island is in Virginia, two miles from the town of Chincoteague. Here, you can swim and canoe (on the bay side), dig for clams, fish, and drive off-road vehicles. The famous wild ponies live on the island, as do many other forms of wildlife. The beach is wild and lovely—you'll find no crowds or hot dog vendors here—and there are numerous trails and observation platforms for viewing the park's many natural wonders.

 George Washington and Jefferson National Forests
5162 Valley Pointe Parkway / Roanoke / 24091
540-265-5100
www.southernregion.fs.fed.us/gwj/

These two national forests cover about 1.6 million acres in Virginia and contain nearly 2,000 miles of hiking trails, including portions of the Appalachian National Scenic Trail. Their website provides a wealth of information about trails, recreation sites, cabins, campgrounds, scenic byways, and more.

 Shenandoah National Park
3655 US 211 East / Luray / 22835
540-999-3500
www.nps.gov/shen

Shenandoah is one of the most visited national parks in the nation. Its 516 miles of hiking trails (including 101 miles of the Appalachian Trail), waterfalls, scenic vistas, wildlife, historic structures, rustic cabins and lodges, and horseback riding offer visitors plenty of opportunities for retreat from city life. One bit of advice, though: You may want to avoid Skyline Drive in October, during peak fall leaf season, if escaping city traffic is what you have in mind. The park is open year-round, although access to Skyline Drive and many visitor services is limited or closed in the winter months. See page 215 for lodging possibilities at the park.

highlight

Driving the Blue Ridge Parkway

One of the most scenic and romantic places for a country drive in Virginia is the Blue Ridge Parkway. There are no traffic lights, 18-wheelers, or billboards to distract you from the breathtaking mountain and valley views. The northern end of the parkway is near Waynesboro, where Skyline Drive ends. The parkway continues south for 469 miles and ends in Great Smoky Mountains National Park in North Carolina.

The parkway, maintained by the National Park Service, has scenic overlooks, picnic tables, restrooms, visitor centers, and camping along the way. A great spot for a picnic is the James River Visitor Center, located near Milepost 60 between Lexington and Roanoke. Here, you can bring a blanket and relax along a lazy river or take a short hike to a restored canal lock and learn about the James River's fascinating past. A bit farther down the road is the Peaks of Otter Visitor Center, which has a popular restaurant on a lovely lake, as well as a lodge for overnight stays (see page 214).

One of the pleasures of the parkway is its immense variety of trees, shrubs, and wildflowers, particularly in the spring and summer. A special time to travel is mid-May to mid-June, when the roadsides are lined with the purple, pink, and white blooms of rhododendron and mountain laurel.

NATIONAL WILDLIFE REFUGES

Detailed information about these and several other national wildlife refuges in Virginia may be found at http://northeast.fws.gov/va.htm.

Mason Neck National Wildlife Refuge
14344 Jefferson Davis Highway / Woodbridge / 22191
703-490-4979

Just a short drive south of Alexandria, you can look for bald eagles, ospreys, and many other forms of wildlife in marshes and forests along the Potomac River. One of the state's largest colonies of blue herons lives at Mason Neck. Canoe tours are available on weekends from April through October. Mason Neck State Park is adjacent to the refuge.

Chincoteague National Wildlife Refuge
P.O. Box 62 / Chincoteague Island / 23336
757-336-6122

The famous Chincoteague ponies live in this protected area on the Virginia side of Assateague Island, located at the northernmost end of Virginia's Eastern Shore. You won't find any hot dog stands here, but you'll enjoy marshes, pine forests, and an especially pristine beach, which is open for day use only. Bird and wildlife watching, biking, and hiking are popular activities; bikes can be rented in the nearby beach resort town of Chincoteague. This is a popular destination, so be sure to book lodging well in advance if you plan to visit between April and September. The annual pony roundup takes place in July.

Eastern Shore of Virginia National Wildlife Refuge
Box 122B / Cape Charles / 23336
757-331-2760

This refuge is at the southern end of Virginia's Eastern Shore, just across the Chesapeake Bay Bridge-Tunnel from the Virginia Beach area. It's a popular spot for bird-watching. Fall is a good time to watch migrating birds passing through the area. The Shore Birding Festival is held here each October.

Rappahannock River Valley National Wildlife Refuge
6610 Commons Drive / Prince George / 23875
804-733-8042 or 804-333-1470

Recent midwinter waterfowl surveys here have counted more than 32,000 ducks, geese, and swans. The refuge also contains wading birds and shorebirds, as well as turkeys in the fields and forest areas.

Back Bay National Wildlife Refuge
4005 Sandpiper Road / Virginia Beach / 23456
757-721-2412

highlight

The Wild Horses of Assateague Island

There are two herds of wild horses known as "Chincoteague ponies," one on the Maryland side of Assateague Island and the other on the Virginia side. They are the descendants of domesticated horses brought here by settlers perhaps as early as the 1600s. Today, the 150-horse Virginia herd is owned by the Chincoteague Volunteer Fire Company, which rounds up the horses each July and guides them on a swim across the channel from Assateague to Chincoteague. Some of the foals are then sold at auction, the proceeds going to support the fire company, which has managed the pony swim and sale every summer since 1924. There's an important environmental benefit to the roundup and auction: The horse population is kept in check, preventing overgrazing on the island.

highlight

Ain't No Mountain High Enough

The Shenandoah National Park Association's latest trail guide, Hikes to Peaks and Vistas in the Shenandoah National Park, *describes hikes of varying levels of difficulty to nine high points in the park, all of which offer magnificent views. Each trail is accessible from Skyline Drive. The hikes range in length from 340 feet (to Stony Man) to a 3.4-mile round trip (to Chimney Rock). This and several other park hiking guides are available at the visitor centers and entrance stations; they can also be ordered online at www.snpbooks.org or by calling 540-999-3582.*

This is the place to view migrating snow geese—some 10,000 of which pass through here around December each year—along with a huge variety of ducks. The refuge is also home to several threatened and endangered species, including bald eagles, peregrine falcons, and loggerhead sea turtles. Trails cut through the varied habitats of beach, dunes, woodlands, and marshlands.

 **Great Dismal Swamp
National Wildlife Refuge
P.O. Box 349 / Suffolk / 23434
804-986-3705**

Located in southeastern Virginia on the North Carolina border, this refuge consists of 100,000 acres of forested wetlands that offer bird and wildlife lovers a different kind of experience. Lake Drummond, a natural lake in the heart of the swamp, is open to small boats.

STATE PARKS

Virginia's 34 state parks are rated among the best in the country. The state parks system claims that no matter where you are in Virginia, you're within an hour's drive of at least one state park. All offer an easy escape from daily life and a chance to get back to the basics, whether you choose to camp for a week or picnic, boat, or hike for a day. For more details about each state park, go to www.dcr.state.va.us/parks.

 Sky Meadows State Park
11012 Edmonds Lane /
Delaplane / 20144
540-592-3556

Located on the eastern side of the Blue Ridge Mountains, this park is less than an hour's drive west of the Virginia suburbs of Washington, D.C. Hiking is popular here; access to the Appalachian Trail is nearby. Much of the park is open pasture that offers beautiful views of the mountains.

 Mason Neck State Park
7301 High Point Road / Lorton /
22079
703-550-0960

This park adjoins Mason Neck National Wildlife Refuge (see page 60).

 Westmoreland State Park
1650 State Park Road /
Montross / 22520
804-493-8821

Explore Park

This 1,100-acre nonprofit educational park along the Roanoke River is devoted to preserving Virginia's cultural heritage and environmental richness. Its outdoor living-history museum features programs on Native American village life and various aspects of colonial life. The park offers opportunities for hiking, mountain biking, canoeing, kayaking, and fishing. Rental equipment is available through a park outfitter. It's possible to be married in the old church on the park grounds, to rent a horse-drawn carriage, and then to have your reception at the Brugh Tavern or in the modern welcome center. Explore Park, located near Roanoke at Milepost 115 of the Blue Ridge Parkway, may be contacted by writing P.O. Box 8508 / Roanoke / 24014, by calling 800-842-9163 or 540-427-1800, or by visiting www.explorepark.org.

This is a great spot for fossil hunting. Shark teeth and whale bones are found frequently along the park's mile and a half of Potomac River shoreline. The amenities here include a swimming beach and a pool. The Horsehead Cliffs rise 150 feet above the shore.

Hughlett's Point Natural Area
State Route 605 / Kilmarnock / 22482
804-462-5030

Wetlands, undeveloped beaches, and upland forests make this park a favorite wintering spot for migrating birds. Bald eagles, ospreys, and northern harriers live here. Viewing platforms, trails, and a woodlands boardwalk make the area accessible to visitors.

Kiptopeke State Park
3540 Kiptopeke Drive / Cape Charles / 23310
757-331-2267

Located on the Chesapeake Bay on Virginia's Eastern Shore across the bay from Norfolk, this park is a favorite with bird watchers, who observe hawks, kestrels, ospreys, and many other species of resident and migratory birds. It also has a beach and a swimming area.

---

highlight

Natural Chimneys Regional Park

Where else in the world can you watch a jousting tournament take place against a backdrop of seven limestone chimneys that resemble ancient castle towers? Dating back to 1821, the tournament is said to be the oldest continuously running sporting event in the United States. The unusual geologic formation that provides a setting for the jousting was created when a cavern rooftop collapsed eons ago and left columns of harder rock standing.

The park, located near Mount Solon between Harrisonburg and Staunton, is open year-round; call 540-249-5729 for tournament dates and details.

First Landing State Park
2500 Shore Drive / Virginia Beach / 23451
757-412-2300

This is the spot where the English settlers landed in 1607. Today, it's a busy place—the most visited state park in Virginia. You can rent equipment for watersports, learn about sea life by visiting the three indoor aquariums, picnic, hike, and more.

 False Cape State Park
4001 Sandpiper Road / Virginia Beach / 23456
757-426-7128

To reach the mile-wide barrier spit that this park sits on, you must enter by foot, bike, or boat through Back Bay National Wildlife Refuge. This has been called one of the last undisturbed coastal environments on the East Coast. Primitive camping is available.

 Caledon Natural Area
11617 Caledon Road / King George / 22485
540-663-3861

Caledon, a National Natural Landmark on the Potomac River, was created to preserve the habitat for a large population of bald eagles. Today, it is home to one of the largest summering populations on the East Coast.

 Lake Anna State Park
6800 Lawyers Road / Spotsylvania / 22553
540-854-5503

Popular with campers, hikers, boaters, and picnickers, this large lake offers something unusual: an abandoned 1800s gold mine. In the summer, the park sponsors programs on panning for gold.

 Pocahontas State Park
10301 State Park Road / Chesterfield / 23838
804-796-4255

This park's proximity to Richmond has made it one of the most visited of all the Virginia state parks. It is a local favorite for biking and picnicking.

 Bear Creek Lake State Park
929 Oak Hill Road / Cumberland / 23040
804-492-4410

Tucked inside Cumberland State Forest, this little-visited park features a 40-acre lake with a boat launch, as well as a beach and picnic and camping areas.

 James River State Park
Route 1, Box 787 / Gladstone / 24553
434-933-4355

This park is relatively new and fairly primitive; no water is available in the campground. It does, however, offer 20 miles of trails for hiking, biking, and horseback riding. Visitors can bring a canoe or kayak and paddle in the James River or pack a picnic lunch and hike to an overlook to view the confluence of the James and Tye Rivers.

 Holliday Lake State Park
Route 2, Box 622 / Appomattox / 24522
434-248-6308

Fishing in the park's lake is a popular activity here. You'll also find plenty of hiking trails winding through Appomattox-Buckingham State Forest.

Smith Mountain Lake State Park
1235 State Park Road /
Huddleston / 24104
540-297-6066

This park sits on one small part of the huge, man-made Smith Mountain Lake, the second-largest lake in Virginia. Fishing and boating are the top activities here, but there are many miles of hiking trails as well.

Fairy Stone State Park
967 Fairystone Lake Drive /
Stuart / 24171
276-930-2424

Named after the unusual "fairy stones" found here, this scenic park in the Blue Ridge foothills about an hour's drive south of Roanoke is one of the oldest and largest in the state parks system. The stones, which are shaped like crosses, are made of brown staurolite. The park has a lovely lake and miles of trails.

Shenandoah River State Park
P.O. Box 235 / Bentonville / 22610
540-622-6840

This new state park stretches along 5.6 miles of the Shenandoah River's south fork between Front Royal and Luray, not far from the northern entrance to Skyline Drive and Shenandoah National Park. Canoeing and tubing are the main activities here; rentals are available from several local outfitters. Horseback riding is also offered through a park concessionaire; call 800-270-8808 for information.

Douthat State Park
Route 1, Box 212 / Millboro / 24460
540-862-8100

Convenient to Lexington and Roanoke, Douthat was rated one of the nation's 10 best state parks by a national magazine a few years back. Built in the 1930s, it is listed on the National Register of Historic Places. Many of the beautiful original buildings—including a full-service restaurant with a view of the lake—are still in use.

Claytor Lake State Park
4400 State Park Road / Dublin / 24084
540-643-2500

A 21-mile-long lake is the center of activity here. Claytor Lake offers the only full-service marina in the state parks system.

Hungry Mother State Park
2854 Park Boulevard / Marion / 24354
276-781-7400

Located just off I-81, this uncrowded park has plenty of hiking trails, a 108-acre lake, campgrounds, and rental cabins.

Grayson Highlands State Park
829 Grayson Highland Lane / Mouth of Wilson / 24363
276-579-7092

You can climb to the top of Virginia's highest peak, Mount Rogers, from this lovely state park in southwestern Virginia. If you go in the spring, you'll be treated to displays of rhododendron on your way up—and you may run into a wild pony or two. Grayson Highlands offers picnicking and horseback riding. You can lodge your horse in the park's horse campground or rent a horse through Hopes and Dreams Unlimited; call 800-899-6554 for information. The Virginia Creeper Trail, popular with both hikers and bicyclists, begins about 10 miles from the park in Whitetop and ends 33 miles later in Abingdon.

 **Wilderness Road State Park**
Route 2, Box 115 / Ewing / 24248
276-445-3065

This new state park sits on a stretch of Daniel Boone's Wilderness Road through the Cumberland Gap, an important route for settlers traveling west in the late 1700s. The 1876 Karlan Mansion can be rented for weddings and other events. The park is five miles east of Cumberland Gap National Historical Park in Middlesboro, Kentucky.

Romantic Getaway

THE NORTHERN NECK

An easy day trip from the D.C. area or from Richmond, Norfolk, or Fredericksburg, Virginia's Northern Neck—the Chesapeake Bay peninsula bounded by the Rappahannock and Potomac Rivers—has a remote and timeless look about it, making it a perfect place to truly get away. Gloucester's historic downtown draws visitors to the courthouse green. Irvington is an upscale riverside village in the middle of rural Virginia. Places like Urbanna and Reedville, fishing towns for centuries, have managed to hold on to their old-time feel.

THINGS TO DO

- ♥ Pick berries and other fresh produce at Westmoreland Berry Farm and Orchard (see page 190)
- ♥ Take a self-guided walking tour of historic Gloucester
- ♥ Visit Popes Creek Plantation, where George Washington was born (see pages 132-33)
- ♥ Shop for antiques in Kilmarnock
- ♥ Walk, picnic (you can order box lunches from Kelsick Gardens in Gloucester), or bird-watch on one of several Potomac River beaches: Colonial Beach (the largest), Westmoreland State Park (see pages 63-64), Hughlett's Point Natural Area (see page 64), VirMar Beach on the Potomac north of Reedville, or Westland Beach near White Stone
- ♥ Tour historic buildings like Christ Church near Irvington, built in 1735, and Stratford Hall, Robert E. Lee's birthplace (see page 133)
- ♥ Sip a glass of wine at Ingleside Plantation Vineyards (see page 182)
- ♥ Take a cruise to Smith Island or Tangier Island in the Chesapeake Bay (see page 92)

- Bicycle through the countryside on the 200-mile-long Northern Neck Heritage Trail
- Play golf at the famous Tides Inn Golden Eagle course (see page 106)
- Visit the Reedville Fishermen's Museum (see page 142) to learn about the work of the watermen
- Hike and bird-watch at Rappahannock River Valley National Wildlife Refuge (see page 61)
- Look for bald eagles at Caledon Natural Area (see page 65)
- Stroll along Millionaire's Row, a string of elegant Victorian houses in Reedville, once one of America's most prosperous towns

PLACES TO EAT

- The Tides Inn / Irvington (see page 204)
- The Trick Dog Café / Irvington (see page 166)
- Kelsick Gardens / 6604 Main Street / Gloucester / 23061; 804-693-6500
- Any seafood restaurant on Tangier Island or Smith Island
- The Inn at Montross / 21 Polk Street / Montross / 22520; 804-493-0573
- Elijah's / 729 Main Street / Reedville / 22539; 804-453-3621

PLACES TO STAY

- The Tides Inn / Irvington (see page 204)
- The Hope and Glory Inn / Irvington (see page 205)
- Inn at Warner Hall / Gloucester (see page 206)
- The Inn at Levelfields / Lancaster (see page 204)

FOR MORE INFORMATION

- Northern Neck Tourist Council / P.O. Box 1707 / Warsaw / 27572; 800-453-6167; www.northernneck.org

Zoos

You don't need to be a kid, or to take a kid, to feel like a kid again. Visiting one of the state's zoos is sure to provide a nostalgic and different kind of day trip.

Virginia Zoological Park
3500 Granby Street / Norfolk / 23504
757-624-9937
www.virginiazoo.org

The zoo's newest exhibit is a re-creation of Africa's Okavango Delta, complete with rhinos, elephants, zebras, lions, giraffes, and monkeys in 10 acres of natural settings. The zoo houses more than 300 animals representing more than 100 species.

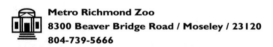

Metro Richmond Zoo
8300 Beaver Bridge Road / Moseley / 23120
804-739-5666

This relatively new and growing zoo was once a private collection. It contains more than 400 animals, including a white Siberian tiger, lions, giraffes, zebras, gazelles, kangaroos, ostriches, camels, lemurs, and many, many monkeys—about 150 of them. All exhibits are outdoors in natural settings. The zoo is located about 30 miles southwest of downtown Richmond off US 360; be sure to call for directions. It's closed on Sundays.

Mill Mountain Zoo
Mill Mountain Park, P.O. Box 13484 / Roanoke / 24034
540-343-3241
www.mmzoo.org

This zoo is home to more than 170 animals, including five endangered species: the Amur tiger, the red wolf, the snow leopard, the white-naped crane, and the clouded leopard.

Romantic Getaway

ABINGDON

Abingdon, in deep southwestern Virginia off I-81 just north of the Tennessee border, was founded in 1778. The oldest town west of the Blue Ridge, it is now a Virginia Historic Landmark. Shops, galleries, and beautiful old homes and gardens fill the 20-block historic district.

THINGS TO DO

- Attend a Broadway play or musical at the famous Barter Theatre (see page 22)
- Take a walking tour of the historic district
- Watch artists at work in a renovated train station at the Arts Depot (see page 32)
- Visit the shops and galleries in the downtown historic district
- Enjoy the Virginia Highlands Festival (see page 54) during the first two weeks in August
- Hike, bike, or horseback ride on an old railroad bed turned into the Virginia Creeper Trail (see pages 69 and 221)
- Hike to the top of Mount Rogers, Virginia's highest peak, from Grayson Highlands State Park (see page 69), or camp and hike at Hungry Mother State Park (see page 68)
- Visit the galleries and exhibits at the William King Regional Arts Center (see page 29)
- Shop till you drop for home decorative items at the 100,000-square-foot warehouse of Dixie Pottery

♥ Listen to old-time music at the Carter Family Fold (see page 14)

PLACES TO EAT

♥ The Dining Room at Camberley's Martha Washington Inn (see page 175)
♥ The Tavern (see page 176)
♥ The Starving Artist Café / 134 Wall Street / 24210; 276-628-8445

PLACES TO STAY

♥ The Martha Washington Inn (see page 221)
♥ The Summerfield Inn Bed and Breakfast (see page 222)

FOR MORE INFORMATION

♥ Abingdon Convention and Visitors Bureau / 335 Cummings Street / 24210; 800-435-3440; www.abingdon.com

GARDENS

Strolling down a romantic garden path hand in hand with your love is a relaxing and tranquil way to spend time outdoors. Virginia is blessed with a mild climate that makes possible a diverse selection of plants. You can enjoy blooms from spring to fall at parks, arboretums, botanical gardens, and historic homes. Below are a few recommended places. Many of the historic homes listed beginning on page 126 also have notable gardens; among them are Gunston Hall, Woodlawn Plantation, Mount Vernon, Oatlands, Montpelier, and Monticello.

**Meadowlark Botanical
   Gardens**
**9750 Meadowlark Gardens
   Court / Vienna / 22182**
703-255-3631
www.nvrpa.org/meadowlark.html

This 95-acre garden is a welcome respite from the congested Tysons Corner area, located just 10 minutes east. The garden is two miles down Beulah Road, off State Route 7 (Leesburg Pike). Three small lakes, two romantic gazebos, the dramatic new Atrium building, and a variety of trails define this lush, hilly spot and make it a perfect close-in getaway for couples needing a break from the northern Virginia congestion. Azaleas, roses, daylilies, and many other perennials grow along the paved walks. Weddings and other functions can be held here.

highlight

The Gardens of Colonial Williamsburg

Colonial Williamsburg is a gardener's delight. More than 90 gardens are scattered behind or beside the homes and buildings. The gardens, which date to the 1930s, 1940s, and 1950s, reflect the colonial approach to planting flowers and vegetables.

 River Farm
7931 East Boulevard Drive / Alexandria / 22308
800-777-7931 or 703-768-5700
www.ahs.org

River Farm, about four miles south of Alexandria, once belonged to George Washington. It is now the headquarters of the American Horticultural Society. In addition to the mansion house, River Farm features 25 acres of gardens overlooking the Potomac River. Picnics may be brought on to the grounds; the gardens and facilities can be rented for weddings and other special occasions.

highlight

A Special Week of Garden Delights

Usually held during the last week in April, Historic Garden Week in Virginia opens up more than 250 homes and gardens to the public all over the state. A tradition for more than 70 years, it's the oldest house-and-garden show in the nation. For more information and a schedule of events, write the Garden Club of Virginia at 12 East Franklin Street / Richmond / 23219. You can also learn about the event by calling 804-644-7776 or visiting www.VAGardenweek.org.

Norfolk Botanical Garden
6700 Azalea Garden Road /
   Norfolk / 23518
757-441-5830
www.virginiagarden.org

Pick a perfect spring day from mid-April to mid-May to visit this 155-acre garden, and you'll be overwhelmed by the profusion of blooms, from azaleas and rhododendrons to camellias, roses (4,000 of them!), and flowering trees. Norfolk Botanical Garden has been cited as one of the top 10 gardens in the country. The waterway (complete with boat rides) that runs through the grounds is a relaxing way to see everything, but meandering hand in hand through the gardens and open meadows is the favorite thing for couples to do here. An excellent spot for outdoor weddings is the Renaissance Garden, where the queen of Norfolk's International Azalea Festival is crowned each year. The Renaissance Garden's grass terraces and dramatic stone columns and statues form a romantic backdrop for the ceremony.

Lewis Ginter Botanical Garden
1800 Lakeside Avenue / Richmond / 23228
804-262-9887
www.lewisginter.org

From masses of tulips in the spring to colorful daylilies in the summer, this 25-acre garden is a great place to stroll and enjoy nature almost any time of year. There's an Asian garden complete with a Japanese teahouse (a great place for lunch), an island water garden featuring wetland plants, and one of the most diverse (770 species) perennial gardens on the East Coast. The newest addition to the garden is its centerpiece, a fabulous all-glass domed conservatory that houses tropical and subtropical plants. The garden areas and several structures can be rented for weddings, receptions, luncheons, and other special occasions.

Maymont
1700 Hampton Street / Richmond / 23220
804-358-7166
www.maymont.org

Located not far from downtown Richmond, Maymont allows visitors to pretend they're strolling in an Italian garden. Its dramatic wisteria-covered pergola is a favorite wedding spot; see Maymont's website for details. A few steps away, down the hill past the waterfall, is a serene Japanese garden overlooking the James River. There's plenty more to see and do here. You can tour the 1893 stone Victorian mansion or look for wild animals in the 40-acre wildlife park on the grounds, where several species of native Virginia animals live, including bears, bison, deer, foxes, and bobcats. A new nature center offers exhibits that explain the rich ecology of the James River area. Maymont has been owned and operated by the city of Richmond since the 1920s.

Glen Burnie Historic House and Gardens
801 Amherst Street /
Winchester / 22601
888-556-5799 or 540-662-1473
www.glenburniemuseum.org

highlight

Two Good Places to Shop for Plants

Two commercial nurseries in the Shenandoah Valley near Staunton are worth a visit, even if plant buying is not in your plans, for both places have attractive gardens you can tour.

One is André Viette Farm and Nursery in Fishersville, on State Route 608 off US 250 between Staunton and Waynesboro; for directions, call 800-575-5538 or visit www.viette.com. This nationally known grower has one of the largest selections of perennials—in particular peonies and daylilies—on the East Coast.

The other is Buffalo Springs Herb Farm, a few miles west of I-81 at the Raphine exit south of Staunton. Located next to Wade's Mill, a working 1700s gristmill, the formal herb and perennial gardens and restored log buildings offer visitors ideas for their own gardens. Call 540-348-1083 or visit www.buffaloherbs.com.

Like many other lovely gardens in Virginia, Glen Burnie comes with a historic house attached—and, in 2003, the new Museum of the Shenandoah Valley. The house and museum are certainly worth touring, but the 25 acres of gardens are the real draw for nature lovers, and a perfect place for a romantic stroll just a few blocks from Old Town Winchester. There's a charming garden house called the Pink Pavilion; rows and rows of huge old boxwoods; a grand allée of flowering crab apple trees; formal rose, perennial, and vegetable gardens accented with classical garden sculpture; a Chinese garden complete with a pagoda-style teahouse; and a water garden. For something different, you can attend one of the monthly summer tours of the gardens; held at night, the tours are accompanied by musical programs. The gardens can be rented for weddings and photo shoots.

**The State Arboretum of
  Virginia**
**400 Blandy Farm Lane (off
  US 50) / Boyce / 22620**
540-837-1758
www.virginia.edu/~blandy

Part of the University of Virginia's Blandy Experimental Farm (also known as the Orland E. White Arboretum), this peaceful place nine miles east of Winchester boasts the largest collection of boxwoods in North America. It is also home to representatives of half the world's pine species, 28 varieties of dogwoods, the largest grove of ginkgo trees in the Western Hemisphere, and lovely azalea, herb, perennial, and daylily gardens. The arboretum is so large that you can drive through it, but packing a picnic and spending a peaceful afternoon exploring its 170 acres is the romantic way to go. The administration and education facilities are housed in old brick buildings that may have served as slave quarters for the nearby Tuleyries estate. The arboretum hosts several events during the year, including a summer outdoor concert series.

 Boxerwood Gardens
963 Ross Road / Lexington /
   24450
540-463-2697
www.boxerwood.com

Named for the boxer dogs of the original owner, Boxerwood Gardens is a 15-acre paradise of more than 6,000 trees and shrubs, including dwarf conifers, Japanese maples, rhododendrons, azaleas, magnolias, and other trees and shrubs. It's located about two miles west of downtown Lexington.

Romantic Getaway

THE CENTRAL SHENANDOAH VALLEY— STRASBURG TO STAUNTON

Take your time to enjoy this historic and scenic part of Virginia by exiting I-81 and traveling the slower-paced Valley Pike, US 11. There's more than a weekend's worth of activities along this 80-mile stretch, but the listings below will give you an idea of the diverse attractions and activities available.

THINGS TO DO

- Hit the antique shops and galleries that line US 211 in Luray and US 11 in Strasburg, Woodstock, Edinburg, Mount Jackson, and New Market
- Meander, in your car or on bicycles, the valley's picture-perfect country back roads
- Hike the mountain trails in George Washington National Forest (see page 58)
- Spend a lazy summer day canoeing or tubing down the Shenandoah River (see pages 91-92)
- Drive through one of the state's last covered bridges, over the Shenandoah River south of Mount Jackson (see page 84)
- Listen to classical music under the stars on the lawn of the old Orkney Springs Hotel during the Shenandoah Valley Music Festival (see page 11)
- Learn the story of the heroic V.M.I. cadets at the Hall of Valor Civil War Museum in New Market (see pages 147-48)

- Watch a jousting tournament at Natural Chimneys Regional Park (see pages 52 and 64)
- Go underground and visit one of the area's many caves (see page 83)
- Play golf in a mountain setting at one of the valley's many lush courses
- Ski or snowboard at Bryce Resort (see page 109) in Basye near Mount Jackson or at Massanutten Resort (see page 109) near Harrisonburg
- Buy milk in a bottle—with the cream on top—at Shenville Creamery and Garden Market (see page 192)
- Browse the huge collection of old books and magazines at Paper Treasures on US 11 in New Market
- Shop the little stores at the Dayton Farmer's Market, a Mennonite-owned small "mall" on State Route 42 south of Harrisonburg
- Also in Dayton, learn about the valley's past at the Shenandoah Valley Folk Art Museum and Heritage Center (see page 148)
- Buy new books at rock-bottom prices at the Green Valley Book Fair south of Harrisonburg, open selected weeks year-round; call 800-385-0099 or visit www.gvbookfair.com for dates
- Take a Saturday-morning guided walking tour of historic Staunton; call the Historic Staunton Foundation at 540-885-7676 for details
- Experience the realities of early settler life at the Frontier Culture Museum in Staunton (see pages 148-49)
- Tour the house in Staunton where Woodrow Wilson was born (see page 138)
- Admire the original Tiffany stained-glass windows in Staunton's historic Trinity Episcopal Church
- Watch a Shakespeare performance at Staunton's Blackfriars Playhouse (see page 21)
- Listen to the Stonewall Brigade Band in Staunton's Gypsy Hill Park on Monday nights during the summer

♥ Take Exit 205 off I-81, trek down a curvy country road, and visit Rockbridge Winery (see page 186), Wade's Mill (see page 145), and Buffalo Springs Herb Farm (see page 78)

♥ Admire and buy high-quality crafts produced by professional artists from around the state at the Artisans Center of Virginia (see page 31), near Waynesboro

PLACES TO EAT

♥ Joshua Wilton House / Harrisonburg (see page 173)

♥ Bell Grae Inn and Restaurant / Staunton (see page 173)

♥ Mrs. Rowe's Family Restaurant and Bakery / Waynesboro Road (Exit 222 off I-81) / Staunton / 24401; 540-886-1833

♥ Southern Kitchen / US 11 South / New Market / 22844; 540-740-3514

♥ Blue Stone Inn Restaurant / 9107 North Valley Pike, US 11 / Lacey Spring / 22833; 540-434-0535

♥ The River'd Inn / 1972 Artz Road / Woodstock / 22664; 800-637-4561

PLACES TO STAY

♥ Strathmore House Bed and Breakfast / Quicksburg (see page 216)

♥ Joshua Wilton House / Harrisonburg (see pages 216-17)

♥ Inn at Keezletown Road Bed and Breakfast / Weyers Cave (see page 217)

♥ The Sampson Eagon Inn / Staunton (see pages 217-18)

FOR MORE INFORMATION

♥ Shenandoah Valley Travel Association / P.O. Box 1040 / New Market / 22844; 540-740-3132; www.shenandoah.org

Caverns

On a hot summer day—or a dreary, wet winter one—you can escape the weather by visiting one of Virginia's underground scenic wonders.

Crystal Caverns at Hupp's Hill
33231 Old Valley Pike / Strasburg / 22657
540-465-8660
www.waysideofva.com/crystalcaverns/

Skyline Caverns
10334 Stonewall Jackson Highway, P.O. Box 193 /
Front Royal / 22630
800-296-4545 or 540-635-4545
www.skylinecaverns.com

Luray Caverns
970 US 211 West, P.O. Box 748 / Luray / 22835
540-743-6551
www.luraycaverns.com

Endless Caverns
P.O. Box 859 / New Market / 22844
540-896-2283

Shenandoah Caverns
261 Caverns Road / Shenandoah Caverns / 22847
540-477-3115
www.shenandoahcaverns.com

Grand Caverns
5 Grand Caverns Drive, P.O. Box 478 / Grottoes / 24441
540-249-5729

Dixie Caverns
5753 West Main Street / Salem / 24153
540-380-2085
www.dixiecaverns.com

COVERED BRIDGES

Like ferries, covered bridges are a romantic relic of Virginia's past. In days gone by, they were often called "kissing bridges," since they were favorite spots for lovers to meet. Eight still stand in the state, five of which are open to the public and are preserved as historic landmarks.

Meem's Bottom Bridge

This 1894 bridge, located on US 11 a mile south of Mount Jackson, crosses the North Fork of the Shenandoah River.

Humpback Bridge

This 1857 bridge spans the James River in Alleghany County. It is located on US 60 a half-mile east of Covington.

Sinking Creek Bridge

This bridge, constructed around 1916, spans Sinking Creek in Giles County. It is located off State Route 601 between State Route 42 and State Route 700.

Bob White Bridge

This 1921 bridge crosses the Smith River in Patrick County near State Route 8 south of Woolvine.

Jack's Creek Bridge

This 1914 bridge spans the Smith River in Patrick County. It is located on State Route 615 just west of State Route 8, two miles south of Woolvine.

Romantic Getaway

LEXINGTON

Lexington had its beginnings as a college town. The Virginia Military Institute and Washington and Lee University have been here since the early 1800s. They sit next door to each other a short walk from the downtown area. Long on history, Lexington is a popular place to live and retire, thanks to cultural amenities like the Theater at Lime Kiln and outdoor possibilities that include nearby nature trails, river rafting, the unusual (for Virginia) Goshen Pass, and the Blue Ridge Parkway.

THINGS TO DO

- Walk and shop in the historic downtown area
- Hire a horse-drawn carriage to take you for a tour of the town, courtesy of Carriage Tours of Lexington (P.O. Box 1242 / Lexington / 24450; 540-463-5647)
- Partake of Civil War history by visiting the museum at Lee Chapel on the Washington and Lee campus or touring the Stonewall Jackson House downtown
- Explore the austere campus of the Virginia Military Institute, which is home to two museums: the V.M.I. Museum, famous for its rather bizarre display of Stonewall Jackson's horse, and the well-done George C. Marshall Museum (see page 150)
- Walk the Chessie Nature Trail
- Enjoy live music—everything from jazz to bluegrass—at Jordan House, an arts center at the corner of Nelson and Randolph Streets
- Attend a horse show at the Virginia Horse Center (see page 113)
- Grab a picnic lunch at Main Street Market downtown and drive west to Goshen Pass, where you'll think you're in another state

entirely; on a hot summer day, join the folks swimming and sunning in the rocky Maury River

♥ Cruise or hike the Blue Ridge Parkway

♥ Explore the preserved locks of the 1800s-era James River/Kanawha Canal

♥ Rent a canoe, raft, or inner tube and paddle down the Maury River or the James River (see page 91)

♥ Drive south to Natural Bridge and see why Thomas Jefferson wanted to own this unusual geologic formation

♥ Drive north to Steeles Tavern and see the farm where Cyrus McCormick invented the revolutionary Virginia reaper (see pages 149-50)

♥ From there, head west under I-81 past the village of Raphine along the lovely State Route 606 to three destinations: Rockbridge Winery (see page 186); Wade's Mill, a working 1700s flour mill (see pages 78 and 145); and the gorgeous gardens, greenhouse, and gift shop of its next-door neighbor, Buffalo Springs Herb Farm

♥ On a summer weekend night, watch a movie from your car at Hull's Drive-In Theater (see page 21)

♥ Attend an outdoor play or concert at the Theater at Lime Kiln (see page 22)

♥ Take a tour and learn about the delightful variety of trees and plants at Boxerwood Gardens (see pages 79-80)

♥ Pig out on chocolate truffles at the nationally recognized Cocoa Mill Chocolate Company (see page 168)

PLACES TO EAT

♥ Willson-Walker House / Lexington (see pages 173-74)

♥ Southern Inn / Lexington (see page 174)

♥ Maple Hall / Lexington (see page 174)

Places to Stay

- 💜 Stoneridge Bed and Breakfast/Autumn Ridge Cottages / Lexington (see pages 219-20)
- 💜 The Sugar Tree Inn / Steeles Tavern (see page 218)
- 💜 Fort Lewis Lodge / Millboro (see pages 218-19)
- 💜 Inn at Keezletown Road / Weyers Cave (see page 217)

For More Information

- 💜 Lexington/Rockbridge Area Visitor Center / 106 East Washington Street / Lexington / 24450; 540-463-3777; www.lexingtonvirginia.com

Waterfalls

If you think you have to travel to a tropical island for a romantic dip in a waterfall pool, think again. Virginia's mountains are home to some of the prettiest waterfalls anywhere. Several have pools suitable for swimming. A few of the loveliest falls are listed below. A comprehensive guide to these and other falls in the state, complete with directions and photos, can be found at www.aria-database.com/waterfall/other/virginia.html.

Great Falls is located in northern Virginia near Washington, D.C., in Great Falls National Park. Trails and picnic areas line the Potomac River along the falls.

Crabtree Falls is actually five falls that drop a combined

1,200 feet in half a mile, making this the highest waterfall east of the Mississippi River. It's a two-mile hike to the top of the falls, but the view is worth the walk. The trail begins off State Route 56 near Tyro not far from the Blue Ridge Parkway and Wintergreen Resort, south of Charlottesville.

Shenandoah National Park is full of falls. One of the most popular is the series of falls at the end of the Whiteoak Canyon Trail. The trail starts at Skyline Drive near Skyland. Others falls worth a hike are Dark Hollow Falls, South River Falls, Lewis Falls, Rose River Falls, Overall Run Falls, and Doyles River Falls. The Shenandoah National Park Association publishes a hiking guide that will help lead you to its waterfalls; see the sidebar on page 62 for ordering information.

St. Mary's Waterfall is located near the town of Vesuvius not far off the Blue Ridge Parkway south of Staunton in the St. Mary's Wilderness Area of George Washington National Forest. This beautiful waterfall makes for good swimming. It's an easy 2.2-mile hike to get there.

Staton's Falls, near Buena Vista, offers a romantic swimming experience in its many pools.

Roaring Run Falls, in the Eagle Rock Roaring Run Furnace Area of Jefferson National Forest southwest of Lexington, is reached by following the lovely Eagle Rock Roaring Run Trail.

Stony Run Falls is located on a 5.2-mile round-trip trail at Douthat State Park near Clifton Forge.

Fallingwater Cascades, near the Homestead Resort and

Covington on US 220, can be seen from the side of the road. Thomas Jefferson raved about the cascades more than 200 years ago in his book, *Notes on the State of Virginia.*

Fun on the Water

Virginia offers water lovers plenty of options, from tubing and canoeing to bay and ocean cruising. The outfitters listed below can get you ready.

Tubing, Rafting, and Canoeing

Butt's Tubes, Inc.
State Route 671, Harpers Ferry Road / Purcellville / 20132
800-836-9911 or 540-668-9007
www.buttstubes.com

Wildlife Expeditions
721 East Side Drive / Chincoteague / 23336
866-C KAYAKS or 757-336-6811

Calm Waters Rowing
10155 Mary Ball Road / Lancaster / 22503
800-238-5578
www.calmwatersrowing.com

Mattaponi Canoe and Kayak Company
11002 West River Road / Aylett / 23009
800-769-3545
www.mattaponi.com

Tidewater Adventures Kayak Ecotours
110 West Randall Avenue / Norfolk / 23503
757-480-1999
www.tidewateradventures.com

Whale and Dolphin Watching off Virginia Beach

You can watch whales and dolphins right off the Virginia Beach shore, thanks to boat trips offered by the Virginia Marine Science Museum. From early January to early March, the museum takes visitors out to sea to look for humpback whales, which stop over each winter on their southern migration to feed in the Chesapeake Bay. Sightings are not guaranteed, however. From mid-June to early October, the museum offers dolphin-watching boat trips on the catamaran Atlantic Princess. Reservations are required; call 757-437-2628. For details, visit the museum's website at www.vmsm.com and click on "Ocean Excursions."

Wild River Outfitters
3636 Virginia Beach Boulevard
  #108 / Virginia Beach / 23452
757-431-8566
www.wildriveroutfitters.com

Clore Brothers Outfitters
5927 River Road /
  Fredericksburg / 22407
540-786-7749
members.aol.com/clorebros

James River Runners
10082 Hatton Ferry Road /
  Scottsville / 24590
804-286-2338
www.jamesriver.com/intro

James River Reeling and Rafting
Main and Ferry Streets /
  Scottsville / 24590
804-286-4FUN

Richmond Raft Co.
4400 East Main Street /
  Richmond / 23231
800-540-7238 or 804-222-7238
www.richmondraft.com

Adventure Challenge
8225 Oxer Road / Richmond /
  23235
804-276-7600
www.adventurechallenge.com

Front Royal Canoe Co.
US 340, P.O. Box 473 / Front Royal / 22630
540-635-5440
www.frontroyalcanoe.com

Downriver Canoe Company
884 Indian Hollow Road / Bentonville / 22610
540-635-5526
www.downriver.com

 Shenandoah River Outfitters
6502 South Page Valley Road / Luray / 22835
800-622-6632
www.shenandoahriver.com

 Massanutten River Adventures
2185 Mockingbird Lane / Elkton / 22827
540-280-2266
www.canoe4u.com

 James River Basin Canoe Livery
1870 East Midland Trail / Lexington / 24450
540-261-7334 or 540-463-9383
www.CanoeVirginia.com

 New River Adventures, Inc.
1007 North Fourth Street / Wytheville / 24382
276-228-8311

Bay, River, and Lake Cruising

 Potomac Riverboat Company
205 The Strand / Alexandria / 22314
703-684-0580
www.potomacriverboatco.com

 Rappahannock River Cruises
US 17 / Tappahannock / 22560
800-598-2628

 Smith Island and Chesapeake Bay Cruises
382 Campground Road, Route 1, Box 289R / Reedville /
 22539
804-453-3430
www.eaglesnet.net/smithislandcruises.com

highlight

Rollin' on the River

Believe it or not, several river ferries still operate in Virginia. The Jamestown-Scotland Ferry, run by the Virginia Department of Transportation, is free. The Hampton-Norfolk Harborlink carries commuters and tourists across the Elizabeth River. The ferry that runs between Reedville and Tangier Island carries passengers only, as does the ferry between Onancock and Tangier Island. White's Ferry takes cars back and forth between Leesburg, Virginia, and Poolesville, Maryland. The free Sunnybank Ferry can take two cars at a time across the Little Wicomico River near Smith Point. The Merry Point Ferry will take you across the Corrotoman River south of Lancaster. One of the two remaining poled ferries in the United States, Hatton Ferry operates from April to November on the James River near Scottsville. For more information on all of these ferries, visit www.virginiadot.org/comtravel/ferry.asp.

Tangier and Chesapeake Cruises
468 Buzzards Point Road /
Reedville / 22539
804-453-2628

Tangier Island Cruise
Hopkins & Bros. Store, 2 Market
Street / Onancock / 23417
757-787-4478

***Miss Hampton II* Harbor Cruises**
710 Settlers Landing Road /
Hampton / 23669
800-800-2202

Harbor Cruise
917 Jefferson Avenue /
Newport News / 23607
800-362-3046 or 757-245-1533

American Rover Tallship Cruises
P.O. Box 3125 / Norfolk / 23514
757-627-SAIL

***Spirit of Norfolk* at Waterside**
Marina
208 East Main Street, Suite 200 /
Norfolk / 23510 (mailing
address)
757-625-1463

***Bianca* Boat-and-Breakfast**
Tidewater Yacht, 10 Crawford
Parkway, Dock A, Slip 22 /
Portsmouth / 23704
800-599-7659 or 757-625-5033

Carrie B Harbor Tours at Waterside (Norfolk)
1238 Bay Street / Portsmouth / 23704 (mailing address)
757-393-4735

Discovery Cruise
600 Laskin Road / Virginia Beach / 23451
757-422-2900

Bateau River Explorations
1795 Avon Street Extended /   Charlottesville / 22902
434-973-8642

This boat is a little different. A bateau is a barge-like vessel used in the 1700s and 1800s in Virginia to haul farm produce and other cargo to market. The trips offered by this company take visitors along a portion of the old James River and Kanawha Canal.

Annabel Lee Riverboat Cruises
4400 East Main Street / Richmond / 23219
800-752-7093 or 804-644-5700

Virginia Dare Paddle Wheel Cruise (on Smith Mountain Lake)
Route 1, Box 140 / Moneta / 24121
800-721-DARE

highlight

Ocean Cruises from Virginia Ports

At least two commercial oceangoing cruise lines—Carnival Cruise Lines (www.carnival.com) and Clipper Cruises (www.clippercruises.com)— depart from Norfolk and Alexandria. Destinations include Bermuda, the Bahamas, and Canada. Cruise schedules change frequently, so check with your travel agent or the cruise-line websites for the latest information.

HIGH-IN-THE-SKY ADVENTURES

Up, up, and away—how romantic can you get? A hot-air balloon ride may be a once-in-a-lifetime event, so you should share it with someone you love. Some real romantics even get married up there. And a ride in a biplane can be a unique and memorable gift for an adventuresome friend or spouse. Of course, for the truly daring, there are hang gliding and skydiving.

Hot-Air Balloon
and Biplane Rides _____

Balloons Unlimited, Inc.
2946-O Chain Bridge Road, Hunter Mill Shopping Center /
   Oakton / 22124
703-281-2300 or 540-554-2002 (balloon port)
www.balloonsunlimited.com

This company has been in business since 1976. It offers hot-air balloon rides of all kinds from its farm in Middleburg.

Flying Circus Airshow
State Route 644 / Bealeton (mailing address: 1900
   Ferguson Lane / Jeffersonton / 22724)
540-439-8661
www.flyingcircusairshow.com

On Sundays from May through October, the Flying Circus Airshow features skydivers, stunt pilots, and wing walkers, who entertain the crowds on the ground. For a price, you can fly in a biplane after the show or schedule an early-morning or late-afternoon hot-air balloon ride. A hot-air balloon festival is held here in August. Bealeton is southwest of Warrenton.

Bonaire Charters Hot Air Balloon Flights
P.O. Box 1092 / Troy / 22974
434-589-5717
www.bonairecharters.com

If you're staying at one of several select bed-and-breakfasts in and around Charlottesville, Bonaire will pick you up and take you on an unforgettable early-morning or early-evening flight that features spectacular views of the Blue Ridge.

Bear Balloon Corporation
231 Turkey Ridge Road / Charlottesville / 22903
800-932-0152 or 434-971-1757
www.2comefly.com

Imagine floating high above the Virginia Piedmont for an hour at sunrise, then enjoying champagne at the Boar's Head Inn afterward. Flights are offered from April through December. Reservations are necessary.

Blue Ridge Hot Air Balloons
552 Milldale Hollow Road / Front Royal / 22630
540-622-6325
www.rideair.com

If you'd like to see the Shenandoah Valley and the Blue Ridge Mountains from a different perspective, then follow up your adventure with a champagne or sparkling apple cider toast, this may be the outing for you.

Virginia Balloons
P.O. Box 388 / Basye / 22810
800-942-7513 or 540-856-3337
www.virginiaballoons.com

highlight

A (Somewhat) Romantic Gift Idea

Many men, and perhaps a few women, would be thrilled to receive a gift certificate good for a flight on a World War II AT-6 fighter trainer. Not only do recipients get to experience the thrill of acrobatic maneuvers in a small plane, but they have a chance to take the controls and fly the plane themselves—with an experienced pilot right there, of course. Rides are offered weekdays only out of the Winchester Airport. For more information, contact Fighter Command / 177 Skyview Lane / Front Royal / 22630. You can reach Fighter Command by phone at 800-809-5482 or 540-635-2203 or visit its website at www.giftflight.com.

This company, which serves the Shenandoah Valley and is planning to expand to the Tidewater area, offers honeymoon, birthday, and bed-and-breakfast packages. Its 12-passenger Love Song balloon is perfect for celebrating weddings and anniversaries.

Hang Gliding

Your love may take you to new heights emotionally, but it's a good bet you've never physically soared through the air without being in an airplane. If you're feeling adventurous, consider learning to hang glide. The following Virginia companies claim it's safe, fun, and exhilarating.

 Silver Wings, Inc.
6032 North 20th Street /
**   Arlington / 22205**
703-533-1965
www.silverwingshanggliding.com

Silver Wings offers lessons in both Virginia and Maryland.

 High Peak Hang Gliding
P.O. Box 4372 / Lynchburg / 24502
804-401-3434
www.davismick.com/highpeak/

Blue Sky
P.O. Box 212 / Penn Laird / 22846
540-432-6557
www.blueskyhg.com

This company offers lessons near Richmond and Harrisonburg.

Skydiving———————————————————————

Would you jump out of a plane to prove your love? If you must, do it with one of these professional skydiving companies. First-time skydivers are welcome at all locations. If you elect to try the tandem diving option, the instructor will hold you in his/her arms as you and your parachute float down to earth.

Hartwood ParaCenter
194 Cropp Road / Fredericksburg / 22406
540-752-4784
www.skydivingcenter.com

Skydive Orange, Inc.
138 Hickory Hill Drive / Fishersville / 22939
877-DIVE SKY
www.skydiveorange.com

This company's dives take place at the town of Orange.

Skydive Virginia! Inc.
P.O. Box 414 / McGaheysville / 22040
540-967-3997
www.skydivevirginia.com

This company's dives take place in Louisa County.

West Point Skydiving Adventures, LLC
708 West Glebe Road / Alexandria / 22305
804-304-9954 (weekdays) or 804-785-9707 (weekends)
www.skydivewestpoint.com

This company's dives take place at the town of West Point.

Adrenaline Air Sports
711 Progress Street / Blacksburg / 24060
540-296-1100
www.air-sports.com

BICYCLING

Virginia is one of the best states in the nation for bicycling and mountain biking. *The Virginia Bicycling Guide* gives information about on-road, off-road, and way-off-road adventures throughout the state. It's published by the Virginia Department of Transportation and the Virginia Tourism Corporation; call 800-835-1203 or request a copy through www.virginiadot.org. The website contains useful information and links on biking in Virginia.

Listed below are a few of the many bicycle touring and outfitting companies around the state.

Old Dominion Bicycle Tours
3620 Huguenot Trail / Powhatan   / 23139
888-296-5036 or 804-598-1808

Shenandoah Mountain Touring
135 South Main Street / Harrisonburg / 22801
877-305-0550 or 540-437-9000
www.mtntouring.com

This company offers mountain-bike tours in George Washington National Forest near Harrisonburg. Its River Valley Road Tours pass along the Shenandoah and Bull Pasture Rivers.

 Alleghany Outdoor Center
P.O. Box 843 / Hot Springs / 24445
888-752-9982 or 304-536-3596

The center arranges mountain-bike tours in Bath, Alleghany, and Greenbrier Counties. It also rents canoes and kayaks.

 New River Bicycles, Ltd.
Route 1, Box 175 / Pulaski /
24324
540-980-1741

 New River Trail Outfitters
451 West Main Street,
P.O. Box 919 / Fries / 24330
276-744-0188

 Bike Station
501 East Main Street /
Damascus / 24236
866-475-3629 or 276-475-3629

 Adventure Damascus Tours and
Bike Shop
128 West Laurel Avenue,
P.O. Box 1113 / Damascus /
24236
888-595-BIKE or 276-475-6262

The two Damascus companies listed above arrange trips on the Virginia Creeper Trail; see the sidebar on page 221 for a description.

highlight

Bike to a Bed-and-Breakfast in Northern Virginia

An organization called the Tri-State Bike Trail Group lets bicyclists plan extended trips on bike trails through Virginia, Maryland, and West Virginia without having to worry about heading home every night. A network of bed-and-breakfasts and inns throughout the region offers hospitality, a secure place to store bikes, shuttle services, and a civilized way to spend the night. Information is available from the Norris House Inn / 108 Loudoun Street SW / Leesburg / 20175. You can call the inn at 800-644-1806 or visit its website at www.norrishouse.com/bikes.

Sports and
Sporting
Events

Come, my Celia, let us prove
While we may the sports of love;
Time will not be ours forever.

Ben Jonson

Watching or playing sports together can be a great shared experience, especially if both of you love the sport in question. Of course, if you hate football but go to the game out of love, well, that's romantic in its own way. Golf is a great game for couples to play together, because, frankly, if only one person plays, the other person may be spending a lot of time alone. If one of you needs to improve your game to make things more fun, consider attending golf school together; several are listed in this section.

Please note that the outdoor activities of hiking, bicycling, and canoeing are covered in "The Great Outdoors" chapter.

GOLF

Virginia has more than 200 golf courses in settings as diverse and beautiful as the state itself, from bays and the ocean to rivers, lakes, meadows, and mountains. The official Virginia tourism website, www.virginia.org, provides descriptions, contact information, and directions for each course. It also publishes the *Virginia Golf Guide*, available free at visitor centers around the state or by phone at 800-932-2259 or email at info@virginia.org. The guide features descriptions of the best courses, announcements of new courses, and information about golf schools, golf-course communities, the weather, and driving distances. Below is its selection of the "Great 18" holes to play in Virginia. For tee times, call the numbers shown, unless noted otherwise.

Bull Run Country Club, hole number 9
3520 James Madison Highway / Haymarket / 20169
877-753-7770 or 703-753-7777
www.bullruncc.com

Stonewall Golf Club, hole number 15
15601 Turtle Point Drive / Gainesville / 20155
703-753-5101
www.stonewallgolfclub.com

Augustine Golf Club, hole number 2
76 Monument Drive / Stafford / 22554
540-720-7374
www.augustinegolf.com

Tides Inn Golden Eagle, hole number 5
480 King Carter Drive / Irvington / 22480
800-843-3746, 804-438-5000, or 804-438-5501 (tee times)
www.the-tides.com/golf

Bay Creek Golf Club, hole number 3
1 Clubhouse Way / Cape Charles / 23310
866-482-4653 or 757-331-9000
www.baycreekgolfclub.com

Golden Horseshoe Gold Course, hole number 16
401 South England Street / Williamsburg / 23185
800-648-6653 or 757-220-7696
www.colonialwilliamsburg.com/visit/golf_rec/index.cfm

Ford's Colony Country Club, Blackheath Course, hole number 18
240 Ford's Colony Drive / Williamsburg / 23188
800-334-6033 or 804-258-4130 (tee times)
www.fordscolony.com/golf

Kingsmill River Course, hole number 17
1010 Kingsmill Road / Williamsburg / 23185
800-832-5665 or 757-253-1703
www.kingsmill.com/golf.html

Heron Ridge Golf Club, hole number 9
2973 Heron Ridge Drive / Virginia Beach / 23456
757-426-3800
www.heronridge.com

Tournament Players Club at Virginia Beach, hole number 2
2500 Tournament Drive / Virginia Beach / 23456
877-484-3872 (ext. 11 for tee times) or 757-563-9440
www.tpc.com/daily/virginia_beach

Birdwood Golf Course, hole number 14
Boars Head Inn, 200 Ednam Drive / Charlottesville / 22903
800-476-1988, 434-296-2181, or 434-293-GOLF (tee times)
www.boarsheadinn.com/bgc.asp

---

highlight

The Really Old Course in Hot Springs

The Old Course at the Homestead Resort opened as a six-hole course in 1892, not long after the first golf courses in the United States were built in the late 1880s. It lays claim to the oldest continuously used first tee in the world. Today, the resort has three golf courses. The Lower Cascades was designed by Robert Trent Jones in 1963. The classic Cascades course has been the site of many national tournaments, including seven USGA championships.

Other longtime Virginia golf courses include Lonesome Pine in Big Stone Gap, which opened in 1924; Shenvallee in New Market, which began play in 1927; and Ocean View, which was built in Norfolk in the 1930s.

Wintergreen Stony Creek,
   hole number 6
Wintergreen Resort, P.O. Box
   706 / Wintergreen / 22958
800-266-2444 (lodging and
   reservations) or 434-325-8250
   (tee times)
www.wintergreenresort.com/golf

highlight

Walk with the
Pros in Virginia

*Couples who love golf can
watch their favorite pros play
during the Michelob Championship at Kingsmill Resort's
River Course in Williamsburg,
held each October. Call 757-
253-3985 for dates and ticket
information.*

Hunting Hawk Golf Club, hole
   number 18
15201 Ashland Road /
   Glen Allen / 23059
804-749-1900
www.huntinghawkgolf.com

Shenandoah Valley Golf Club,
hole number 9
134 Golf Club Circle, Route 2,
   Box 1240 / Front Royal / 22630
540-636-4653
www.svgcgolf.com

Caverns Country Club, hole number 1
P.O. Box 748 / Luray / 22835
888-443-6551 (tee times) or 540-743-7111
www.luraycaverns.com/pages/luray%20golf.html

Homestead Cascades, hole number 18
Homestead Resort, US 220, Main Street, P.O. Box 2000 /
   Hot Springs / 24445
800-838-1766 or 540-839-1766
www.thehomestead.com

The River Course, hole number 18
8400 River Course Drive / Radford / 24141
540-633-6732
www.rivercoursegolf.com

Lonesome Pine Country Club, hole number 15
State Route 610 / Big Stone Gap / 24219
276-523-0739

GOLF SCHOOLS

Golf is a terrific sport for couples because tee placements and the handicap system help even things out between men and women. Learning to play well can make the game more fun, so why not spend your spring or summer vacation at one of Virginia's resort golf schools?

 Kingsmill Resort Golf Academy
1010 Kingsmill Road / Williamsburg / 23185
800-832-5665, 757-253-1703, or 757-253-3998
www.kingsmill.com

Kingsmill offers individual lessons, golf clinics, a one-day golf school, a golf/spa package, and a multiday package, which includes accommodations, all meals, and use of the resort. Classes run from February through October.

 **The Colonial Golf Academy**
P.O. Box 356 / Williamsburg / 23187
800-566-6660 or 757-566-1600
www.golfcolonial.com/academy.html

Sessions are held year-round and are one to four days long. Participants receive four hours of instruction each day. Rates include use of the practice course and reduced greens fees. Accommodations are not provided, but lodging is plentiful in and around Williamsburg.

Wintergreen Golf Academy
Wintergreen Resort, P.O. Box 706 / Wintergreen / 22958
800-266-2444 or 434-325-8250 (golf information)
www.wintergreenresort.com

Three- and five-day sessions are offered from April through October. Packages include lodging, lunch, cart and greens fees, and other resort amenities.

The Homestead's Golf Advantage School
US 220, Main Street, P.O. Box 2000 / Hot Springs / 24445
800-838-1766
www.thehomestead.com

Participants receive group or individual instruction in all areas of the game. Packages include accommodations, all meals, cart and greens fees, and other resort amenities. The school operates from April through October.

SKIING AND SNOWBOARDING

Virginia has four ski resorts: Bryce and Massanutten in the central Shenandoah Valley; Wintergreen, near Charlottesville; and The Homestead in the southern Shenandoah Valley. All four depend on snowmaking equipment, so even if natural snowfall has been scarce, call to see if the slopes are open. All offer downhill skiing, snowboarding, and other snow-related outdoor activities, as well as lodging and ski packages.

Wintergreen Resort
P.O. Box 706 / Wintergreen / 22958
434-325-8057 (ski information)
www.wintergreenresort.com

This resort just off the Blue Ridge Parkway has 20 slopes and trails with five lifts. Its Plunge Snow Tubing Park features a vertical drop of 100 feet and a 900-foot total run. Free lessons are offered to those who rent ski or snowboarding equipment.

Bryce Resort
P.O. Box 3 / Basye / 22810
800-821-1444 or 540-856-2121
www.bryceresort.com

This small, friendly, member-owned resort two hours west of Washington, D.C., is an easy day trip for people in northern Virginia. It offers eight slopes, lessons for all ages, and night skiing. A snow-tubing park is being planned.

Massanutten Resort
P.O. Box 1227 / Harrisonburg / 22803
540-289-9441
www.massresort.com

Snowboarding, ski boarding, and night skiing are available on 14 downhill trails. Snow tubing is a popular activity at Massanutten's recently opened tubing park. Ski lessons are available though the ski school.

The Homestead
US 220, Main Street, P.O. Box 2000 / Hot Springs / 24445
800-838-1766
www.thehomestead.com

In addition to nine downhill trails for skiing and snowboarding, The Homestead offers opportunities for snow tubing, cross-country skiing, snowshoeing, ice skating, guided snowmobile tours, and horse-drawn sleigh rides.

ICE SKATING

When was the last time you put on ice skates? It's probably been awhile. Wouldn't it be romantic to glide on the ice hand in hand with your love? Here are a few fun rinks to try.

Reston Town Center Skating Pavilion
1818 Discovery Street / Reston / 20190
703-709-6300
www.restontowncenter.com

Not far from Washington Dulles International Airport, this popular outdoor rink is the centerpiece of an upscale area that includes shopping, restaurants, a movie theater, and offices. It's open from mid-November through March 10.

Charlottesville Ice Park
230 West Main Street / Charlottesville / 22902
434-817-1423
www.icepark.com

This indoor rink is located at the west end of Charlottesville's historic downtown mall. The University of Virginia hockey team plays its games here, so call for public skating hours.

Richmond Ice Zone
636 Johnston Willis Drive / Richmond / 23236
804-378-7465
www.richmondicezone.com

This indoor rink offers theme nights on Thursday evenings in the summer. Past theme nights have featured music of the sixties, seventies, and eighties.

The Ice Station
3710 Tom Andrews Road NW / Roanoke / 24019
540-265-1505
www.theicestation.com

The Ice Station boasts an NHL-sized indoor ice rink. It offers lessons and public skating sessions all year.

HORSE RACING/STEEPLECHASE

There are two kinds of horse racing in Virginia. In the first, thoroughbred horses run on a flat track, and you sit in the stands, place bets, and hope you have enough money left to buy dinner. The second is steeplechase, a more social affair for which you dress up, bring a sumptuous picnic lunch, sit on the lawn, and watch beautiful horses and highfalutin people (or is it the other way around?).

Morven Park Steeplechase Races
P.O. Box 6228 / Leesburg / 20178
703-777-2414
www.morvenpark.org

highlight

Happy Trails

For a comprehensive guide to scenic horse trails at several parks and forests in Virginia, visit the website of the Virginia Horse Journal at www.virginiahorse.com and click on "Virginia Horse Council," then on "Trails." The guide has links to other horseback-riding and trails sites. The website also features a directory of stables in Virginia.

Each October, this charity event is held on the grounds of the historic Morven Park mansion (see page 126), where horse racing has been a favorite sport since the early 1800s.

Middleburg Spring Races
P.O. Box 1173 / Middleburg / 20118
540-687-6545
www.middleburgspringraces.com

The state's oldest steeplechase event is held each spring at Glenwood Park near Middleburg, the picturesque heart of Virginia's hunt and horse country.

Virginia Fall Races
P.O. Box 2 / Middleburg / 20118
540-687-5662
www.vafallraces.com

This two-day steeplechase event, held every fall since 1955, also takes place at Glenwood Park near Middleburg.

The Virginia Gold Cup and the International Gold Cup
P.O. Box 840 / Warrenton / 20188
800-69-RACES or 540-347-1215
www.vagoldcup.com

Both of these steeplechase events are all-day affairs at Great Meadows, located near The Plains, just off I-66 about an hour's drive west of Washington, D.C. The Gold Cup, which draws up to 45,000 people every May, rain or shine, is as much a social event as a sporting event; it's been held every year since 1922. The International Gold Cup, which takes place each October, attracts a slightly smaller crowd.

Colonial Downs
10515 Colonial Downs Parkway /
   New Kent / 23124
804-966-7223
www.colonialdowns.com

At Colonial Downs, you can spend a day at the races at Virginia's only thoroughbred and harness-racing track with pari-mutuel betting. You can even have your wedding at this plush new facility. New Kent is not far off I-64 between Richmond and Williamsburg. Each spring, usually in April, the Strawberry Hill Races are held here, sponsored by the National Steeplechase Association.

 Foxfield Races
P.O. Box 5187 / Charlottesville /
   22905
434-293-9501
www.foxfieldraces.com

highlight

*The Virginia
Horse Center*

If you like horses, you'll love this huge, modern facility just outside Lexington in the Shenandoah Valley. The Virginia Horse Center holds all kinds of horse shows year-round. The shows average up to 400 horses and 4,000 exhibitors and spectators. Admission is free. For more information, contact the center at P.O. Box 1051 / Lexington / 24450. You can reach the center by phone at 540-463-2194 or visit its website at www.horsecenter.org.

Steeplechases are held here each spring and fall. You can pack a tailgate lunch (don't forget fresh flowers and a candelabra!) and spend the day watching six races and a nattily dressed crowd from one of the hillsides around the course.

 Montpelier Hunt Races
11407 Constitution Highway / Montpelier Station / 22957
540-672-2728
www.montpelier.org

Montpelier was once the home of President James Madison (see pages 134-35). The Montpelier Hunt Races are held each fall, following a tradition set by previous owner Marion du Pont Scott, a famous American horsewoman.

Auto Racing

Watching cars race may not seem romantic to some people, but many Virginians have been loving these exciting events for years. Listed below are the two largest speedways in the state. For website links to 17 other Virginia speedways, go to www.racingaroundamerica.com/speedways/virginia.asp.

Richmond International Raceway
P.O. Box 9257 / Richmond /
**   23227**
804-345-7223
www.rir.com

This raceway attracts crowds of 150,000 to its NASCAR Winston Cup series races each year. From its beginnings on a dirt horse-racing track at the Virginia State Fairgrounds in the late 1940s, it has grown in size and sophistication ever since. It now claims to have more seats than any other Virginia sports complex.

---

highlight

Sports Car and Motorcycle Racing

VIR, the Virginia International Raceway, reopened a few years ago after being closed in 1974. Located near Danville, VIR is now a modern 3.2-mile track for sports car racing. It has 12 major turns, two straights, and 130 feet of elevation change. All kinds of sports cars—old and new—compete here, as do motorcycles. NASCAR drivers often use VIR as a test course. For details and schedules, contact VIR at 1245 Pine Tree Road / Alton / 24520. You can reach the raceway by phone at 888-RACE099 or 434-822-7700 or view its website at www.virclub.com.

Martinsville Speedway
P.O. Box 3311 / Martinsville / 24112
877-722-3849
www.martinsvillespeedway.com

This speedway, which can accommodate 86,000 fans, has been around since 1949, making it one of the country's oldest. The Virginia 500 and other Winston Cup circuit events are held here.

PROFESSIONAL BASEBALL

Virginia doesn't have a major-league baseball team, but it does have several minor-league teams, including two AAA (one step down from the majors) affiliates, the Richmond Braves and the Norfolk Tides. Rooting for the home team on a fine summer evening makes for a wonderfully all-American date.

 Potomac Cannons
7 County Complex Court / Woodbridge / 22912
703-590-2311
www.potomaccannons.com

This Carolina League team is a class A affiliate of the St. Louis Cardinals.

 Norfolk Tides
150 Park Avenue / Norfolk / 23510
757-622-2222
www.norfolktides.com

This International League team is the AAA affiliate of the New York Mets.

Richmond Braves
The Diamond, 3001 North Boulevard / Richmond / 23230
804-359-4444
www.rbraves.com

Part of the International League, the Braves are the AAA affiliate of the Atlanta Braves.

Lynchburg Hillcats
P.O. Box 10213 / Lynchburg / 24506
434-528-1144
www.lynchburg-hillcats.com

The Hillcats, part of the Carolina League, are a class A farm team of the Pittsburgh Pirates.

Danville Braves
P.O. Box 378 / Danville / 24543
434-797-3792
www.dbraves.com

A member of the Appalachian League, the Danville Braves are a rookie farm team of the Atlanta Braves.

Salem Avalanche
P.O. Box 842 / Salem / 24153
540-389-3333
www.salemavalanche.com

This Carolina League team is a class A affiliate of the Colorado Rockies.

Pulaski Rangers
P.O. Box 676 / Pulaski / 24301
540-980-1070
www.pulaskirangers.com

The Pulaski Rangers are a rookie affiliate of the Texas Rangers. They play in the Appalachian League.

 Martinsville Astros
P.O. Box 3614 / Martinsville / 24115
276-666-2000
www.martinsvilleastros.com

The Astros are a rookie affiliate of the Houston Astros. They are an Appalachian League team.

 Bristol White Sox
P.O. Box 1434 / Bristol / 24203
276-669-6859
www.3wave.com/brisox

Part of the Appalachian League, the Bristol White Sox are a rookie team of the Chicago White Sox.

PROFESSIONAL SOCCER

For soccer-loving couples, a great date would be to attend a match featuring one of Virginia's two professional teams.

 Hampton Roads Mariners
Virginia Beach Sportsplex, 2181 Landstown Road /
 Virginia Beach / 23456
757-430-9800
www.hamptonroadsmariners.com

The Mariners are an A-league affiliate of the Colorado Rapids, D.C. United, and the New England Revolution.

Richmond Kickers
2320 West Main Street / Richmond / 23220
804-644-5425
www.richmondkickers.com/

The Kickers are part of the United Soccer League, the official feeder system to major-league soccer in the United States. The team is an A-league affiliate of D.C. United and the Tampa Bay Mutiny.

PROFESSIONAL ICE HOCKEY

Virginia has three minor-league hockey teams, located in the eastern and central parts of the state and in the Shenandoah Valley. People in northern Virginia are closest to the Washington Capitals, a major-league team. If the two of you usually watch this sport on television, you won't regret getting out of the house and experiencing the excitement up close.

Norfolk Admirals
1300 Diamond Springs Road, Suite 101 / Virginia Beach /
23455
757-363-1900
www.norfolkadmirals.com

The Admirals are an American Hockey League team affiliated with the Chicago Blackhawks.

Richmond Renegades
601 East Leigh Street / Richmond / 23219
804-643-7825
www.renegades.com

Roanoke Express
2740 Franklin Road, Suite 3 / Roanoke / 24014
540-343-4500
www.roanokeexpress.com

The Richmond Renegades and the Roanoke Express are minor-league teams of the East Coast Hockey League, an affiliate of the National Hockey League.

COLLEGE SPORTS

Football is the most popular college team sport in Virginia. Two state university teams top the list: the University of Virginia Cavaliers, an ACC team, and the Virginia Tech University Hokies, a Big East team.

To purchase tickets for UVA football (and basketball), visit the Virginia Athletic Ticket Office in Bryant Hall at the Carl Smith Center, off Stadium Road. You may also write P.O. Box 400826 / Charlottesville / 22904 or call 800-542-8821. Schedules and other UVA sports information may be accessed at http://virginiasports.ocsn.com.

For Virginia Tech tickets, contact the Athletic Ticket Office, 401 Cassell Coliseum / Blacksburg / 24061 or call 800-828-3244 or 540-231-6731. Tickets may also be ordered through www.hokiesports.com.

Women's basketball is becoming a hot event in Virginia. Old Dominion University's Lady Monarchs are the top team.

As of 2001, they'd made it into NCAA tournament action for 18 of the past 20 years. For ticket information, call the ODU Athletic Ticket Office at 757-683-4444. Or you can access a ticket order form at http://odusports.ocsn.com and mail it to Old Dominion University Athletic Ticket Office, Athletic Administration Building, Room 124 / Norfolk / 23529.

Romantic Getaway

FREDERICKSBURG

This small city on the falls of the Rappahannock River has been a backdrop to many crucial events in American history. The story begins in the colonial era with the Washington family—George spent part of his childhood here, and his mother, sister, and brother lived here. The Civil War raged in and around Fredericksburg for three years; visitors can tour four battlefields and war-related sites and pick up brochures and information at the Fredericksburg Visitor Center.

THINGS TO DO

- ♥ Take a self-guided walking tour of historic Old Town Fredericksburg
- ♥ Shop the more than 100 shops, boutiques, and galleries of Old Town, including the four-block-long "Antique Row"
- ♥ Stop at the visitor center to pick up information for a self-guided walking tour of 12 public and private Old Town gardens
- ♥ Take a trolley or carriage tour of the town courtesy of Fredericksburg Carriage Tours (1700 Caroline Street / 22401; 540-654-5511)
- ♥ See the art collection inside and the gardens outside at Belmont (see page 27)
- ♥ Admire the lovely interiors and lush gardens at Kenmore (see page

132), the home of George Washington's only sister

♥ Visit other Washington family homes, including Ferry Farm (see page 132), the Mary Washington House, and the Rising Sun Tavern (see page 131)

♥ Visit the area's Civil War battlefields

♥ Pan for gold at Lake Anna State Park (see pages 65-66)

♥ Sun on the beach at Westmoreland State Park (see pages 63-64)

PLACES TO EAT

♥ Bistro 309 (see pages 169-70)

♥ Claiborne's (see page 169)

PLACES TO STAY

♥ The Richard Johnston Inn (see page 208)

♥ The Charles Dick House Bed and Breakfast (see page 208)

FOR MORE INFORMATION

♥ Fredericksburg Visitor Center / 706 Caroline Street / 22401; 800-678-4748 or 540-373-1776

♥ Fredericksburg Area Tourism; 800-654-4118; www.fredericksburgvirginia.net

Romancing
the Past

The past is only the present become invisible and mute; and because it is invisible and mute, its memoried glances and its murmurs are infinitely precious. We are tomorrow's past.

Mary Webb

Virginia—in 1607 the site of the first permanent English settlement on the continent and the largest of the 13 original colonies—is rich in historic places. Visiting them is a great way to sample the romance (and hardships) of life in the past. Mount Vernon and Monticello are obvious destinations, but many historic homes and buildings scattered all over the state are less well known but just as lovely and interesting to visit. In most cases, the enticing gardens of these gracious old places make for a romantic destination in themselves; for other picturesque gardens, see the listings starting on page 74.

For those who want to delve a little deeper into the past, the state's many museums and historic sites document every aspect of Virginia's fascinating past, from prehistoric times to the day before yesterday. Several of the larger and better-known facilities are listed here, but don't bypass the many local museums put together by towns, counties, and historical societies throughout the state. They hold some of the most human and interesting stories of all, and their curators and docents are usually volunteers with a deep connection to their area's past.

Also included in this chapter are the state's top science and nature museums.

Historic Homes and Buildings

Morven Park
17263 Southern Planter Lane / Leesburg / 20178
703-777-2414
www.morvenpark.com

Located just off US 7 northwest of downtown Leesburg, this elegant Greek Revival mansion on 1,200 acres was once the home of Virginia governor Westmoreland Davis, who served in the early 1900s. Morven Park is a landmark of the Virginia hunt country; the Museum of Hounds and Hunting is housed in one of the mansion's wings.

Oatlands Plantation
20850 Oatlands Plantation Lane / Leesburg / 20175
703-777-3174
www.oatlands.org

Oatlands, built in the early 1800s by a great-grandson of colonial Virginian Robert "King" Carter, is a 22-room Greek Revival mansion set in the rolling countryside outside Leesburg. Tours of the house are available, and there are four acres of formal gardens to stroll through as well. Evening weddings in the gardens may be arranged from May through October. Throughout the year, there's always something going on, including equestrian events, sheepdog trials, and dog shows. During the Christmas season, the mansion is open on Saturday evenings for candlelight tours (as are many other homes in this section).

Arlington House, the Robert E. Lee Memorial
Arlington National Cemetery / Arlington
703-235-1530
www.nps.gov/arho/

Now administered by the National Park Service, Arlington House was home to General Robert E. Lee and his family for more than 30 years. It was built by George Washington Parke Custis, Martha Washington's grandson, in the early 1800s. It was here that Robert E. Lee married Mary Custis (Martha's great-granddaughter) in 1831.

Carlyle House Historic Park
121 North Fairfax Street /
Alexandria / 22314
703-549-2997
www.carlylehouse.org

This grand old Palladian manor house in the heart of Old Town Alexandria dates back to 1753, when one of the town's founders, John Carlyle, moved in. It's said that Lord Fairfax and George

---

highlight

The James River Plantations

The Charles City area, located along the James River between Williamsburg and Richmond, is great for exploring some of America's oldest historic sites. The area remains largely rural, making it easy to imagine life in the 1600s and beyond, when Indians, settlers, farmers, and future presidents lived here. Five James River plantation homes are open to the public: Sherwood Forest, Westover, Shirley, Evelynton, and Berkeley. Visit www.jamesriverplantations.org for information and directions; this helpful site also lists a few local restaurants and bed-and-breakfasts, some of which host weddings and other celebrations.

Washington attended gatherings here. Tours are given throughout the day. Groups of fewer than 100 people may rent the gardens for late-afternoon and evening events—including weddings—from April through October.

Woodlawn Plantation and Pope-Leighey House
9000 Richmond Highway, US 1 / Alexandria / 22309
703-780-4000
www.nationaltrust.org

Woodlawn Plantation was built for George Washington's adopted daughter, Nelly Custis, and her husband, Lawrence Lewis, in 1802 on land the president bequeathed to her. It was designed by Dr. William Thornton, the original architect of the United States Capitol.

Nearby sits a more modern historic home, the Pope-Leighey House. Designed by Frank Lloyd Wright, the house is an example of his Usonian style of moderately sized homes. It is full of many architectural ideas that influenced home design in America in the mid-20th century. Built in Falls Church in 1940, it was moved here in 1965, when its existence was threatened by the construction of I-66.

Both properties are owned by the National Trust for Historic Preservation and are located just three miles from Mount Vernon.

Mount Vernon
P.O. Box 110 / Mount Vernon / 22121
703-780-2000
www.mountvernon.org

Open every day of the year, George Washington's home and gardens draw more than a million visitors annually, so schedule your visit accordingly. Weekdays in late fall, winter, and early spring are your best bets. Located about 13 miles south of Alexandria at the southern end of the George Washington Parkway, this is a place every Virginian should visit at least once.

 Gunston Hall
10709 Gunston Road / Mason Neck / 22079
800-811-6966 or 703-550-9220
www.gunstonhall.org

This Georgian brick home was the property of George Mason, one of the framers of the Constitution. Located not far from Mount Vernon, it is well worth a visit. Built in the mid-1700s, it features elaborately carved interior woodwork and a boxwood garden that may date back to Mason's time. The garden areas and the Ann Mason Room in the visitor center may be rented for weddings and other functions.

 **Kerr Place**
69 Market Street / Onancock / 23417
757-787-8012
www.kerrplace.org

Changing exhibits, art shows, garden tours, and holiday candlelight tours are just a few of the events that the Eastern Shore of Virginia Historical Society sponsors at this grand early-1800s brick home in the charming Chesapeake Bay fishing village of Onancock.

 Sherwood Forest Plantation
State Route 5, 14510 John Tyler Highway, P.O. Box 8 /
  Charles City / 23030
804-829-5377
www.sherwoodforest.org

Sherwood Forest was the home of the 10th president of the United States, John Tyler, from 1842 until his death in 1862. It is unusual in that it's still owned and maintained by the president's descendants, who live on the estate. More than 300 feet in length, it is said to be the longest frame house in America. The impressive grounds feature many species of wonderful trees, including the oldest ginkgo tree in America. Weddings, dinners, luncheons, and other events can be held on the grounds and in the Overseer's House. The estate is located between Richmond and Williamsburg.

Berkeley Plantation
State Route 5, 12602 Harrison Landing Road / Charles City /
   23030
804-829-6018
www.berkeleyplantation.com

Not far from Sherwood Forest is another president's home—Berkeley Plantation, where the ninth United States president, William Henry Harrison, was born. This 1726 Georgian mansion and its 10 acres of formal gardens overlooking the James River comprise one of the most beautiful properties in the state. Berkeley is said to be the oldest three-story brick house in Virginia that can prove its date of origin.

Bacon's Castle
State Route 617, P.O. Box 364 / Surry / 23883
757-357-5976
www.apva.org

This handsome house is one of the oldest brick residences in North America. It was built by a planter, Arthur Allen, in 1665 in the Jacobean architectural style. Its name derives from

Bacon's Rebellion, a struggle led by Nathaniel Bacon in 1676 to protest the colony's tyrannical royal governor, William Berkeley. One of Bacon's men used the house as a headquarters for several months, thereby bestowing its name. Bacon's Castle and nearby Smith's Fort Plantation are maintained by the Association for the Preservation of Virginia Antiquities, which owns 23 other historic Virginia properties; see the organization's website for details.

Cape Henry Lighthouse
Fort Story, off State Route 60 / Virginia Beach
757-422-9421
www.apva.org/apva/light.html

This wonderful old octagonal sandstone structure, built in 1791, was in use until 1881. It is open to the public daily in the spring, summer, and fall—that is, if you can make the climb up the steep spiral staircase to the top, 90 feet up. It's the third-oldest lighthouse still standing in the United States and the official symbol of the city of Virginia Beach.

Mary Washington House
1200 Charles Street / Fredericksburg / 22401
800-678-4748 or 540-373-1776
www.apva.org

George Washington bought this white frame house for his mother, Mary Ball Washington, in 1772. She lived here until her death 17 years later. Two other interesting historic properties nearby are the Rising Sun Tavern, at 1304 Caroline Street, built by Charles Washington, the president's youngest brother; and the Hugh Mercer Apothecary Shop, at 1020 Caroline Street, a colonial-era pharmacy.

Kenmore Plantation and Gardens
1201 Washington Avenue / Fredericksburg / 22401
540-373-3381
www.kenmore.org

Built in the 1770s by George Washington's sister, Betty, and her husband, Fielding Lewis, this brick mansion was one of the most elaborately decorated in America. Over the past 10 years, the gardens and grounds have been undergoing restoration to return them to their appearance in the 1700s. Kenmore and Ferry Farm (see below) are being preserved by George Washington's Fredericksburg Foundation.

George Washington's Ferry Farm
State Route 3 East / Fredericksburg (mailing address: 1201
Washington Avenue / Fredericksburg / 22401
540-373-3381, ext. 28
www.kenmore.org

Though the small frame house is long gone, this is the farm where George Washington grew up from the age of six into his teens. George's mother, Mary Ball Washington, lived most of her life at Ferry Farm, located across the Rappahannock River from Fredericksburg.

George Washington Birthplace National Monument
1732 Popes Creek Road, State Route 204 / Washington's
Birthplace / 22443
804-224-1732
www.nps.gov/gewa

Only the outline of the foundation remains from the home where George Washington was born and spent the first three years of his life. Nonetheless, you can tour a reconstruction built in 1932 to commemorate the 200th anniversary of our first president's birth. Located about 40 miles east of Fredericksburg, the land belonged to Washington's great-grandfather, who settled here in the mid-1600s. Today, the 550-acre site is managed by the National Park Service. You can bring a picnic and hike at this lovely place where Popes Creek enters the Potomac River. The family cemetery on the property is worth a visit to see the burial places of Washington's father, grandfather, and great-grandfather.

Stratford Hall Plantation
State Route 214 / Stratford / 22558
804-493-8038 or 804-493-8371 (weekends and holidays)
www.stratfordhall.org

This is Robert E. Lee's birthplace, built by the patriarch of Virginia's illustrious Lee family in the 1730s. House tours are given daily at this lovely brick Georgian mansion situated high above the Potomac River. The house is near Montross, less than an hour's drive southeast of Fredericksburg. It is not far from Popes Creek Plantation, George Washington's birthplace, and other Northern Neck historic sites.

Monticello
P.O. Box 217 / Charlottesville / 22902
434-984-9822
www.monticello.org

Monticello—probably the most famous home in America other than the White House—was a lifelong project of Thomas Jefferson's. He spent 40 years building, tearing down, and improving this architectural jewel. It is the only house in America on the United Nations World Heritage List. The curators are devoted to discovering and preserving the 18th-century plants that Jefferson planted here.

Ash Lawn-Highland
1000 James Monroe Parkway, State Route 795 /
    Charlottesville / 22902
434-293-9539
www.avenue.org/ashlawn

This relatively modest frame farmhouse about two miles down the road from Monticello was the home of President James Monroe and his family for more than two decades. Its beautiful boxwood gardens form the backdrop for the popular Summer Music Festival. *Money* magazine has called the Ash Lawn Opera Festival—sung in English, by the way—one of the world's top 20 warm-weather events (see pages 9-10). Other functions—including private weddings, a spring wine festival, garden tours, and Christmas candlelight tours—are held on the grounds throughout the year. Here's an interesting fact about Monroe, our fifth president: He died on July 4, 1831, five years to the day after Presidents Adams and Jefferson. He is buried in Hollywood Cemetery in Richmond.

Montpelier
11407 Constitution Highway, State Route 20 / Montpelier
    Station / 22957
540-672-2728
www.montpelier.org

This gracious Southern mansion, its exterior painted a lovely peachy pink, is in rural Orange County about 20 miles south of Charlottesville. The original part of the house, built in 1760 by James Madison's father, has been added on to and changed over the decades. Madison was the fourth United States president. He and his wife, Dolley, entertained lavishly here during their retirement years. The extensive grounds include farmland, a formal two-acre garden planted in the style of the early 1900s, and a racetrack where the Montpelier Hunt Races are held each November (see pages 113-14). The James Madison Landmark Forest, which begins behind the house, offers walking trails through 200 acres of old-growth forest.

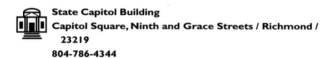

State Capitol Building
Capitol Square, Ninth and Grace Streets / Richmond /
   23219
804-786-4344

Free tours of this Thomas Jefferson-designed building are given every day of the week. Jefferson modeled the State Capitol, a striking example of Classical Revival architecture, after the Roman temple Maison Carrée in Nimes, France, which he visited while serving as ambassador to that country. Inside is a beautiful domed ceiling cleverly hidden within the building's pitched roof. A true-to-life marble sculpture of George Washington by the famous French sculptor Houdon stands in the rotunda.

Agecroft Hall
4305 Sulgrave Road / Richmond / 23221
804-353-4241
www.agecrofthall.com

You don't have to cross the Atlantic to tour a 500-year-old English Tudor house—one was brought to Virginia back in the 1920s. Agecroft Hall was shipped in crates, piece by piece, from Lancashire, England (where a wealthy Richmond man bought it at auction) to its current home on the James River, where it was carefully rebuilt. Today, the house and its formal English gardens are the setting for many programs throughout the year, including the Richmond Shakespeare Festival (see page 20).

 Virginia House
4301 Sulgrave Road / Richmond / 23221
804-353-4251
www.vahistorical.org

This beautiful and impressive English Tudor home, built in 1929 in the Windsor Farms neighborhood of Richmond, is a museum of the Virginia Historical Society. It was constructed partly of materials from a 12th-century English building. Eight acres of formal and natural gardens offer the perfect escape from the bustle of downtown Richmond.

 Poplar Forest
P.O. Box 419 / Forest / 24551
434-525-1806
www.poplarforest.org

Thomas Jefferson frequently visited the Lynchburg area in the years after his presidency to find respite from the constant stream of visitors to Monticello. Poplar Forest, his modest but enchanting octagonal retreat, is undergoing a careful and extensive renovation to restore its original appearance. The house was privately owned until the early 1980s. The work, begun in 1984, is expected to be completed in 2004. Until then, visitors can watch the restoration and archaeological work in progress. The home is open from April through November.

Red Hill
1250 Red Hill Road / Brookneal / 24528
804-376-2044
www.redhill.org

Red Hill was the last home of Patrick Henry, famous American patriot and governor of Virginia. It is also his burial place. The home's Grant Museum Room boasts the largest collection of Henry memorabilia in the world. The modest white clapboard house is a careful reconstruction of the original, built on the same foundation. Brookneal is 35 miles southeast of Lynchburg.

Historic Long Branch
P.O. Box 241 / Millwood / 22646
888-558-5567 or 540-837-1856
www.historiclongbranch.com

This lovely brick manor home, built by Tidewater tobacco magnate Robert Carter Burwell in the early 1800s, is beautifully situated on a wide, rolling meadow with spectacular views of the Blue Ridge in the distance. Its graceful spiral staircase alone is worth the visit. The home was extensively restored and tastefully furnished in the late 1980s by its last owner, who established a trust before his death in 1990 that allowed the mansion to be open to the public. Tours are given on weekend afternoons from April through October. Long Branch is a bit off the beaten path, at the intersection of State Route 624 and State Route 626 near Millwood (a great place to shop for antiques, by the way). The mansion may be reserved for weddings and other special events.

Belle Grove Plantation
336 Belle Grove Road / Middletown / 22645
540-869-2028
www.bellegrove.org

Belle Grove, on US 11 between Strasburg and Middletown, was built of local limestone in 1797 for a son of one of the first settlers in the Shenandoah Valley, Major Issac Hite. It was a huge and impressive house for its day. Hite's wife, Nelly, was the sister of James Madison. The story goes that James and Dolley Madison spent part of their honeymoon here in an earlier house on the property. During the Civil War, Belle Grove found itself in the middle of the Battle of Cedar Creek. Today, the National Trust for Historic Preservation cares for this beautiful old home, which is open to the public for guided tours.

Woodrow Wilson Birthplace and Museum
18-24 North Coalter Street / Staunton / 24402
540-885-0897
www.woodrowwilson.org

Just up the hill from historic downtown Staunton, in a tree-lined neighborhood of lovely old homes, is the house where Woodrow Wilson, the 28th president of the United States, was born. The adjacent museum describes the highlights of Wilson's life and presidency and features his favorite car, a 1919 Pierce-Arrow limousine, which was donated to the museum by Wilson's widow, Edith Bolling Galt Wilson. The Garden Club of Virginia restored the lovely 1933 boxwood garden behind the house.

Romantic Getaway

ALEXANDRIA

The Old Town historic district of Alexandria is a delightful place to spend a day or a week—there's plenty to see and do. This 1700s port city sits along the Potomac River just south of Washington, D.C. Its two Metro subway stations make it a convenient base for visiting the many attractions in the nation's capital.

THINGS TO DO

- ♥ Walk, walk, walk the lovely tree-lined streets of Old Town and admire the many beautifully restored old homes and gardens
- ♥ Take a Potomac River boat ride to Georgetown or Mount Vernon (see pages 128-29)
- ♥ See artists at work at the Torpedo Factory Art Center (see page 29), and visit the Alexandria Archaeology Museum while you're there
- ♥ Ride bicycles or take long walks along the Potomac on the Mount Vernon Trail, which runs for more than 18 miles from the Mount Vernon estate to D.C.'s Theodore Roosevelt Island
- ♥ Listen to live country music at the Birchmere (see page 8)
- ♥ Shop the boutiques, galleries, and antique stores—there are dozens—and enjoy eating at the many good and varied restaurants
- ♥ Pack a lunch with goodies from one of Old Town's gourmet food stores and head a few miles south to picnic in the gardens of River Farm (see page 75)
- ♥ Travel back to the past by visiting historic sites like Christ Church, where George Washington and Robert E. Lee were once members;

learn about Alexandria's past at The Lyceum (see page 141); tour Robert E. Lee's boyhood home (see page 133) and his later home, Arlington House (see page 127); tour Carlyle House (see pages 127-28); or take a walking tour—self-guided or guided—from the 1720s Ramsay House Visitors Center at 221 King Street

♥ Head south a few miles on the George Washington Parkway to visit several other historic homes: Mount Vernon (see pages 128-29), Gunston Hall (see page 129), and Woodlawn Plantation and the Pope-Leighey House (see page 128), designed by Frank Lloyd Wright

♥ Hike and look for bald eagles and other wildlife at Mason Neck State Park (see page 63)

PLACES TO EAT

♥ Elysium (see page 165)
♥ La Bergerie (see page 165)
♥ Le Gaulois (see page 165)
♥ Gadsby's Tavern Restaurant / 138 North Royal Street / 22314; 703-548-1288
♥ The Majestic Café / 911 King Street / 22314; 703-837-9117

PLACES TO STAY

♥ Morrison House (see pages 201-2)
♥ Most national chain hotels

FOR MORE INFORMATION

♥ Ramsay House Visitors Center / 221 King Street / 22314; 800-388-9119 or 703-838-4200; www.funside.com

HISTORIC SITES AND HISTORY MUSEUMS

 Alexandria Archaeology Museum
Torpedo Factory Art Center, 105 North Union Street /
   Alexandria / 22314
703-838-4399
www.AlexandriaArchaeology.org

Housed in the Torpedo Factory, an old munitions factory that now serves as the city's Potomac-side arts center, this museum is worth a visit to reflect on Alexandria's long and interesting past. More than 2,000 artifacts from the 2-million-piece collection are on display, including old shoes, gloves, and stockings that were found preserved in the water of wells and privies. Among the many glass and ceramic items is the largest collection of Staffordshire ware on the continent. The museum is located near Old Town's many shops and restaurants.

 **The Lyceum**
201 South Washington Street / Alexandria / 22314
703-838-4994
www.alexandriahistory.org

Located in Old Town, this elegant 1839 building tells the rich history of Alexandria, which was founded in 1749.

 **Kinsale Museum On-the-Green**
Kinsale Road, P.O. Box 307 / Kinsale / 22488
804-472-3001

The village of Kinsale, founded in 1706, claims to be the oldest seaport on the Virginia side of the Potomac. From the 1860s to the 1930s, it was a busy market town and steamboat port. The museum tells its story and also offers a walking-tour guide to this picturesque town from the past.

Reedville Fishermen's Museum
504 Main Street / Reedville / 22539
804-453-6529
www.rfmuseum.com

If you've never heard of menhaden, a fish important to this part of Virginia, you can learn all about it here. This charming museum relates the life of the area's watermen and features exhibits of several boats from the early 1900s. You can also pick up a guide for a walking tour of Reedville.

Colonial Williamsburg
134 North Henry Street / Williamsburg / 23185
800-HISTORY or 757-229-1000
www.colonialwilliamsburg.org

Travel back to the time when Williamsburg was Virginia's bustling capital and experience the customs, architecture, gardens, and way of life in the big city during colonial times. Although a bit of a tourist trap, this outdoor museum has much to offer. It is an especially romantic place to visit during the holiday season, when old-fashioned lights and decorations add to its appeal.

Jamestown Settlement and Yorktown Victory Center
P.O. Box 1607 / Williamsburg / 23187
888-593-4682 or 757-253-4838

The site of the first permanent English settlement in America and the location of the decisive battle of the American Revolution are practically next door to each other. Two museums tell the story. Jamestown Settlement is just 10 minutes from Colonial Williamsburg, and the Yorktown Victory Center is another 10 minutes down the road. Both museums are run by the Jamestown-Yorktown Foundation.

 Colonial National Historical Park
P.O. Box 210 / Yorktown / 23690
757-898-2410 or 757-229-1733
www.nps.gov/colo/home.htm

Stretching along the tree-lined, 23-mile Colonial Parkway, which connects Jamestown, Williamsburg, and Yorktown, this 9,000-acre park includes Jamestown National Historic Site, Yorktown National Battlefield, Yorktown National Cemetery, and Cape Henry National Memorial. It is run by the National Park Service. Park rangers are on hand to give interpretive tours.

 The Mariners' Museum
100 Museum Drive / Newport News / 23606
757-596-2222
www.mariner.org

Devoted to the history of the sea, this museum's collection includes ship models, maritime art, scrimshaw, figureheads, and steam engines. Among the subjects covered are the age of exploration and the ships and watermen of the Chesapeake Bay.

 **Nauticus, the National Maritime Center**
1 Waterside Drive / Norfolk / 23510
800-664-1080 or 757-664-1000
www.nauticus.org

This large, modern facility on Norfolk's waterfront is a science and technology museum devoted to the sea. The second floor is occupied by the Hampton Roads Naval Museum, which covers the maritime history of the area since the Revolutionary

War. On the third floor, the National Oceanic and Atmospheric Administration (NOAA) has an exhibit on the data that helps guide ships in United States waters. The USS *Wisconsin* is docked next to Nauticus. There is no charge to walk the decks of this World War II battleship.

James Monroe Museum and Memorial Library
908 Charles Street / Fredericksburg / 22401
540-654-1043
http://departments.mwc.edu/jmmu/www/

Mary Washington College runs this state-owned museum

highlight

By the Old Mill Stream

Virginia is blessed with several wonderful old gristmills, a few of which are still grinding away. Visiting one is a fun way to get a taste of life in the old days. Below are a few that are open to the public.

Aldie Mill
P.O. Box 322 / Aldie /
20105
703-327-9777

This 1807 mill is on US 50 in the village of Aldie, near Middleburg.

Colvin Run Mill
10017 Colvin Run Road /
Great Falls / 22066
703-759-2771

On the first and third Sundays in the spring, summer, and fall months, you can watch flour and corn being ground at this 1811 mill, located on US 7 west of Tysons Corner.

George Washington's
Grist Mill
P.O. Box 110 / Mount
Vernon / 22151
703-780-2000

This 1770 mill is located three miles south of Mount Vernon.

full of fascinating information about our fifth president. It features a large collection of Monroe family artifacts, including the desk on which he wrote what became known as the Monroe Doctrine. One of the more romantic exhibits is Elizabeth Monroe's beautiful amethyst tiara and matching bracelets, acquired when James Monroe was the United States minister to France.

Valentine Museum / Wickham House
1015 East Clay Street / Richmond / 23219
804-649-0711
www.valentinemuseum.com

Burwell-Morgan Mill
15 Tannery Lane, P.O.
Box 282 / Millwood /
22646
540-837-1799

Call for grinding times at this beautifully restored 1785 mill.

Wade's Mill
55 Kennedy-Wade's Mill
Loop / Raphine / 24472
800-290-1400 or
540-348-1400
www.wadesmill.com

This mill was constructed around 1750. Flour and corn are still ground here today; call for hours of operation and grinding times.

Mabry Mill
266 Mabry Mill Road
SE, Milepost 176 /
Meadows of Dan /
24120
276-952-2947

This early-1900s mill is located at Milepost 176 on the Blue Ridge Parkway near the Meadows of Dan.

White's Mill
12291 White's Mill
Road / Abingdon /
24210
276-676-0285

This is the only water-powered gristmill left in southwestern Virginia. It dates to the late 1700s. Today, it grinds cornmeal.

This museum, not far from the State Capitol, documents Richmond's history with permanent and changing exhibits. The property includes the elegant and historic Wickham House, built in 1812 by a wealthy local lawyer, John Wickham, who is remembered for successfully defending Aaron Burr in his treason trial; tours of the house are offered, and its gardens are available for weddings. The Garden Café at the Wickham House serves breakfast and lunch.

Edgar Allen Poe Museum
1914 East Main Street / Richmond / 23223
888-21-EAPOE
www.poemuseum.org

One of the world's largest collections of material related to the author Edgar Allen Poe is housed in the Old Stone House in Richmond's Shockoe Bottom district. The museum is a few blocks from the first home Poe lived in during his years in the city. Poe loved gardens. Weddings may be held in the museum's intimate Enchanted Garden.

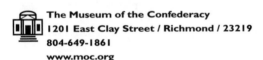
The Museum of the Confederacy
1201 East Clay Street / Richmond / 23219
804-649-1861
www.moc.org

This fine Civil War museum displays thousands of artifacts, including the swords of Generals Lee and Jackson, flags, weapons, uniforms, art, and photographs. It is located next door to the restored 1818 mansion known as the White House of the Confederacy, where President Jefferson Davis and his family lived from 1861 to 1865.

The Museum of Virginia History
428 North Boulevard / Richmond / 23220
804-358-4901
www.vahistorical.org

"The Story of Virginia," this museum's permanent exhibit, covers 16,000 years of the state's past. Changing exhibits have included shows of art, photography, and architecture relating to Virginia and Virginians. The museum, in the headquarters of the Virginia Historical Society, is conveniently located right next door to another popular Richmond museum, the Virginia Museum of Fine Arts (see page 28).

National D-Day Memorial
202 East Main Street / Bedford / 24523 (foundation office)
800-351-3329 or 540-586-3329
www.dday.org

The little town of Bedford suffered the nation's worst loss in relation to its population on D-Day in 1944, when 23 of its sons died on the Normandy beaches and in the days that followed. Dedicated in 2001, this is the national monument to D-Day in the United States. It's an outdoor memorial located on the outskirts of Bedford, which is between Lynchburg and Roanoke.

Hall of Valor Civil War Museum
P.O. Box 1864 / New Market / 22844
540-740-3101

Part of New Market Battlefield State Historical Park, located alongside I-81, this museum documents the Civil War in the Shenandoah Valley. Special emphasis is placed on the legendary Battle of New Market, in which 257 students from the Virginia Military Institute helped the Confederates to victory.

 Virginia Quilt Museum
301 South Main Street / Harrisonburg / 22801
540-433-3818

This museum focuses on the role of quilts and quilting in cultural life. Work by early and contemporary quilt artisans is displayed.

 Shenandoah Valley Folk Art Museum and Heritage Center
Bowman and High Streets, P.O. Box 716 / Dayton / 22821
540-879-2681
www.heritagecenter.com

Here you can see furniture, quilts, pottery, baskets, and guns crafted by the region's original German and Scots-Irish settlers and learn about the history of the valley from Native American days to the present. One of the popular permanent exhibits is a large electric map and accompanying audio program that describes General Stonewall Jackson's Valley Campaign of 1862.

 Frontier Culture Museum
US 250, P.O. Box 810 / Staunton / 24402
540-332-7850, ext. 124
www.frontiermuseum.org

Four farmhouses dating from the 1600s to the 1800s are the main attractions at this nonprofit outdoor living-history park. The three farmhouses brought from Germany, England, and Ireland represent homes typical of immigrants from those countries. The fourth is from the Shenandoah Valley. Docents dressed in period attire explain and demonstrate practices from daily life in years gone by. The museum is near Exit 222 off I-64/I-81.

 McCormick Farm
Shenandoah Valley Agricultural Research and Extension
   Center, Cyrus McCormick Circle / Steeles Tavern / 24476
540-377-2255

This farm, now operated by Virginia Tech, was the site of the birthplace and workshop of Cyrus McCormick, inventor in 1831 of the world's first successful mechanical reaper, a machine that

highlight

Things That Go Bump in the Night

Though not everyone thinks that walking around old neighborhoods in the dark looking for ghosts is romantic, it certainly can bring couples closer together. Regularly scheduled ghost tours are held in at least four of Virginia's old towns: Alexandria, Occoquan, Leesburg, and Lexington. Many other towns sponsor ghost-related events around Halloween.

In Alexandria, tours start from the garden of the Ramsay House, the town's visitor center, located at 221 King Street, at 7:30 P.M. and 9:00 P.M. on Fridays and Saturdays and at 7:30 P.M. on Sundays from mid-March through November. Call 703-838-4200 for more information.

In Occoquan, a river town along the Potomac south of Alexandria,

ghost tours are offered occasionally throughout the year by Historic Occoquan; call 703-491-5984 for information.

In Leesburg, a self-proclaimed "paranormal investigator" leads ghost tours through the historic district. The tours begin at 17 South King Street at 7:00 P.M. on Fridays and Saturdays from May through November; call 703-913-2060 to confirm day and time.

In Lexington, ghost tours are given nightly from late May through Labor Day and on weekends through October. Reservations are necessary. Call Ghost Tours of Lexington at 540-348-1080.

moved agriculture into the modern age. Several structures, including a gristmill and a blacksmith's shop (which houses a small museum of McCormick's inventions) are open to the public. The farm is located on State Route 606 between I-81 (Exit 205) and US 11.

 **George C. Marshall Museum**
P.O. Drawer 1600, V.M.I. Parade / Lexington / 24450
540-463-7103
www.marshallfoundation.org

This interesting museum focuses on the life and times of George C. Marshall, a 1901 Virginia Military Institute graduate who won the Nobel Peace Prize in 1953. Marshall served as general of the army in World War II and later led the effort to carry out a relief plan—the Marshall Plan—to aid war-devastated Europe.

 **Virginia Museum of Transportation**
303 Norfolk Avenue / Roanoke / 24016
540-342-5670
www.vmt.org

The state's official transportation museum is located in the historic Norfolk & Western freight station in downtown Roanoke. Exhibits include a large collection of diesel locomotives and rail vehicles, as well as many old automobiles, trucks, and fire engines.

 **History Museum and Historical Society of Southwestern**
   Virginia
Center in the Square, 1 Market Square / Roanoke / 24011
540-342-5770
www.history-museum.org

This museum covers southwestern Virginia history from prehistoric times to the present. Its interesting collection focuses on daily life in the past. If you're a movie and theater buff, you'll enjoy the Theatre History Gallery, which contains costumes and memorabilia gathered from the 23 live theaters and movie theaters that once operated in town.

Blue Ridge Institute and Museum
P.O. Box 1000, Ferrum College / Ferrum / 24088
540-365-4416
www.blueridgeinstitute.org

This is the state center for Blue Ridge folklore. Its exhibits and programs honor Virginia's rich cultural traditions, from music to decorative arts and crafts. The Blue Ridge Folklife Festival, held each October, features live music and regional folk artisans (see page 53).

Southwest Virginia Museum Historical State Park
P.O. Box 742 / Big Stone Gap / 24219
276-523-1322
www.dcr.state.va.us/parks/swvamus.htm

This museum, housed in an 1880s mansion built by a former Virginia attorney general, documents the area's settlement and growth from the 1700s, back when Daniel Boone blazed the Wilderness Road through nearby Cumberland Gap.

Romantic Getaway

WILLIAMSBURG

Colonial Williamsburg is probably the state's most famous tourist attraction, so be prepared for crowds almost any time of year. It's probably at its romantic best during the winter holiday season, when the historic area is wrapped in old-fashioned decorations and lit by candles at night.

THINGS TO DO

- ♥ Spend the day roaming the 173-acre outdoor living-history museum known as Colonial Williamsburg (see page 142), which offers more than 500 historic buildings, costumed interpreters, and working colonial craftsmen

- ♥ Visit the Yorktown battlefield (see page 147), where the American Revolution was won

- ♥ Walk the grounds at Jamestown (see pages 142-143), the site of the first permanent English settlement in America

- ♥ Take a scenic ride on the Jamestown-Scotland Ferry (see page 92)

- ♥ Browse the upscale shops at Merchants Square in Colonial Williamsburg, or hit one of the outlet strip malls in town

- ♥ Play golf at three of the state's top courses: the Golden Horseshoe, Ford's Colony Blackheath, and the Kingsmill River Course (see pages 104-5)

- ♥ Stroll the campus of William and Mary, the nation's second-oldest university

- ♥ See a fine collection of American folk art at the Abby Aldrich Rockefeller Folk Art Museum and other decorative arts at the DeWitt Wallace Decorative Arts Museum (see page 27); both are in Colonial Williamsburg

- ♥ Relive our colonial past by visiting the James River plantation estates of Berkeley, Sherwood Forest, Westover, Shirley, and Evelynton near Charles City (see pages 127-30), as well as Bacon's Castle in Surry (see pages 130-31)
- ♥ Learn about Virginia terra and fauna at the Virginia Living Museum (see page 157)
- ♥ Learn about life at sea at the Mariners' Museum (see page 147)
- ♥ Ride the scary Alpengeist roller coaster or see a show at Busch Gardens Williamsburg, a beautifully landscaped European-themed amusement park
- ♥ Bet on the horses at Virginia's only pari-mutuel thoroughbred racetrack, Colonial Downs in New Kent (see page 115)

PLACES TO EAT

- ♥ The Trellis Café (see page 167)
- ♥ The Dining Room at Ford's Colony (see page 167)

PLACES TO STAY

- ♥ The many lodging choices available through Colonial Williamsburg (see page 206)
- ♥ Numerous chain hotels
- ♥ The Fife & Drum Inn (see page 206)
- ♥ Kingsmill Resort (see pages 206-7)

FOR MORE INFORMATION

- ♥ Williamsburg Area Convention and Visitors Bureau; 800-368-6511; www.visitwilliamsburg.com

SCIENCE MUSEUMS

Virginia Living Museum
524 J. Clyde Morris Boulevard / Newport News / 23601
757-595-1900
www.valivingmuseum.org

The Washington Post described the Virginia Living Museum as being "full of things that wriggle, jump, glide and flutter," especially as regards species native to Virginia and the surrounding region. The museum's indoor and outdoor attractions include a wildlife park, a botanical preserve, an aviary, a science museum, an aquarium, and a planetarium.

Virginia Air & Space Center
600 Settlers Landing Road / Hampton / 23669
757-727-0900
www.vasc.org

Located in downtown Hampton, this museum is also the visitor center for NASA's Langley Research Center. Exhibits include the Apollo 12 command capsule, a moon rock, a Mars meteorite, a space shuttle landing simulator, and several historic airplanes and helicopters. An IMAX theater shows films on many topics. The museum also offers the Cosmic Carousel, a restored turn-of-the-20th-century merry-go-round.

Virginia Marine Science Museum
717 General Booth Boulevard / Virginia Beach / 23451
757-425-3474
www.vmsm.com

Featuring 800,000 gallons of aquariums, an outdoor aviary, a nature trail, and 10 acres of marsh habitat, this museum is a terrific place to learn about the state's marine ecology. You can see live sharks, seals, otters, and stingrays and take seasonal whale- and dolphin-watching boat trips. The museum is home to the only 3-D IMAX theater in Virginia; marine and nature films are shown on its six-story-high screen. Yes, you'll have to wear the funny 3-D glasses.

Chesapeake Planetarium
Chesapeake Municipal Center, P.O. Box 15204 / Chesapeake / 23328
757-547-0153 or 757-547-STAR (recorded message)
www.chesapeake.va.us

The planetarium offers free educational programs for the public one night a week; call for topics and dates.

Leander McCormick Observatory
University of Virginia Astronomy Department,
P.O. Box 3818 / Charlottesville / 22903
434-924-7494
www.astro.virginia.edu

This observatory, located on the campus of the University of Virginia, is open to the public for stargazing certain nights of the month; see the calendar on the website for dates.

Science Museum of Virginia
2500 West Broad Street / Richmond / 23220
800-659-1727 or 804-864-1400

Although this museum's many hands-on exhibits are aimed at children, adults can learn a lot as well, on topics ranging from space, chemistry, computers, and electricity to life sciences, telecommunications, crystals, and physics. It's also fun to watch a 70 mm movie on the state's largest film screen and see a planetarium show at the museum's IMAX Dome and Planetarium.

 **Science Museum of Western Virginia and Hopkins
Planetarium
Center in the Square, I Market Square / Roanoke / 24011
540-342-5710
www.smwv.org**

Much like the Science Museum of Virginia in Richmond, this museum is aimed at kids but provides grownups plenty to learn and enjoy. The 750-gallon Hardbottom Reef Tank is home to a variety of corals, sea sponges, and fish that live in the reefs off the Atlantic coast of the United States. The huge wraparound screen at the MegaDome Theater shows nature and science films, including IMAX titles that make you feel like you're on the scene. The planetarium features multimedia astronomy shows for all ages.

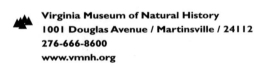 **Virginia Museum of Natural History
1001 Douglas Avenue / Martinsville / 24112
276-666-8600
www.vmnh.org**

This state museum offers exhibits, programs, and field trips on all sorts of natural-history topics, from wild animals to rocks to dinosaurs to Virginia wildflowers. One long-term museum project is the excavation of a fossil whalebone bed at the Carmel Church Quarry in Caroline County.

Romantic Getaway

WINCHESTER

Winchester is one of Virginia's oldest towns. Today, it's one of the state's fastest-growing. Lovely old brick and stone homes run for blocks along tree-lined streets in the historic district, and the surrounding rolling countryside is covered with apple and peach orchards. In the spring and summer especially, this is a great area for driving country roads and picking up local produce at roadside stands.

THINGS TO DO

- ♥ Walk the shaded gardens of historic Glen Burnie (see pages 77-78)
- ♥ Pack a picnic and explore the extensive grounds of the State Arboretum of Virginia (see pages 78-79), located a few miles east
- ♥ Stroll and shop or have lunch on Old Town's pedestrian mall
- ♥ Pick up a self-guiding walking-tour map of the historic district at the Kurtz Visitor Center downtown and relive the fascinating history of the town where George Washington once lived and worked, as did Stonewall Jackson for a while during the Civil War
- ♥ Take a cooking class at the Terra Cotta Kitchen (see page 180)
- ♥ Drive south a few miles to Middletown and tour historic Belle Grove Plantation (see page 138), then treat yourself to a tasty snack from the Route 11 Potato Chip Company; stay the evening and enjoy a play at the historic Wayside Theatre (see pages 20-21)
- ♥ Watch a movie at the Family Drive-In (see page 21) on US 11 in Stephens City
- ♥ Go antique hunting in three directions: south on US 11 to Strasburg, east on US 50 to Millwood, and north on US 11 to Inwood and Martinsburg, West Virginia

- ♥ Tour the exquisitely furnished 1800s mansion called Long Branch (see page 137), located near Millwood; don't miss the Shenandoah Valley Hot Air Balloon and Wine Festival, held here in October (see page 52)
- ♥ Head west on US 50 for a country drive over lush mountains into West Virginia

PLACES TO EAT

- ♥ Violino Ristorante Italiano / Winchester (see page 172)
- ♥ The Cheese Board / 147 North Loudoun Street / Winchester / 22601; 540-667-3168
- ♥ One Block West / 25 South Indian Alley / Winchester / 22601; 540-662-1455
- ♥ Terra Cotta Kitchen / Creekside Station, 3031 Valley Avenue, US 11 / Winchester / 22601; 540-723-8800
- ♥ Café Sofia / 2900 Valley Avenue, US 11 / Winchester / 22601; 540-667-2950
- ♥ L'Auberge Provençale / White Post (see page 172-73)
- ♥ The Wayside Inn / 7783 Main Street / Middletown / 22645; 877-869-1797

PLACES TO STAY

- ♥ The Inn at Vaucluse Spring / Winchester (see page 215)
- ♥ L'Auberge Provençale / White Post (see page 172-73)

FOR MORE INFORMATION

- ♥ Winchester-Frederick County Convention and Visitors Bureau; 800-662-1360 or 540-662-4135; www.visitwinchesterva.com

Wining
and
Dining

I prefer not to have among my guests two people or more, of any sex, who are in the first wild tremours of love. It is better to invite them after their new passion has settled, has solidified into a quieter reciprocity of emotions. (It is also a waste of good food, to serve it to new lovers.)

M. F. K. Fisher

The restaurants in this section were chosen for couples who are looking for places to celebrate special occasions or to go on a special date. From formal to funky, each restaurant in its own way offers a romantic setting and good food that should make for a night to remember. Note that many of these restaurants have websites with photos and sample menus, allowing you to get an idea of selections and prices before you go.

This chapter also lists some other food- and wine-related activities for couples to enjoy, including cooking classes, wineries, and places to find fresh Virginia farm products. Food and wine festival listings begin on page 37.

Restaurants

Dinner in the Garden
42461 Lovettsville Road, State Route 672 / Lovettsville /
  20180
540-822-9017
www.patowmackfarm.com/dinners.html

And now for something completely different: Your dining room is under a big white tent-top in a farm garden with a view of the Potomac River, and your meal is made with fresh organic ingredients grown here and on farms nearby. This is the special treat offered from late April to early November by Patowmack Farm, an organic farm that sells seasonal produce and packaged organic food items in its country store. The five-course fixed-priced dinners are served on alternate Fridays and Saturdays; reservations are required. Patowmack Farm is a 15-minute drive from Leesburg.

Lightfoot Restaurant
11 North King Street / Leesburg / 20176
703-771-2233
www.lightfootrestaurant.com

Housed in a beautiful old 1880s bank building in the historic downtown area of Leesburg, this friendly restaurant, a local favorite, has a highly rated wine list and is open for lunch (reasonably priced) and dinner (a little more expensive).

L'Auberge Chez François
332 Springvale Road / Great Falls / 22066
703-759-3800
www.aubergefrancois.com

This country restaurant has long been a Washington-area favorite for romantic dates and celebrations. Getting here is just as romantic, as guests travel a long, winding, tree-lined road. The service is friendly, the atmosphere country French (picture little red-shaded lamps on the tables) but not stuffy, the service professional but not snooty, and the food always good. Reservations are essential; call four weeks in advance.

Black Coffee Bistro
101 South Madison Street / Middleburg / 20118
540-687-3632

Housed in a 1790s clapboard house, this charming restaurant serves modern American fare in a serene, romantic setting. It offers lunch, dinner, and Sunday brunch. Reservations are suggested.

Colvin Run Tavern
8045 Leesburg Pike / Tysons Corner / 22182
703-356-9500
www.kinkead.com

This classy new restaurant is owned by Chef Bob Kinkead, famed for his Kinkead's restaurant in Washington, D.C. Located across the street from the Tysons Corner mall and next to Tiffany and Gucci, Colvin Run Tavern is not really a tavern, but rather four modern, sophisticated, serene small dining rooms featuring some of the best food and service in northern Virginia. One national magazine has called it a "restaurant worth building a trip around."

highlight

Meals on Wheels

Relive (if you were born by then) the nostalgic 1950s by flashing your headlights for curb service at one of the state's few surviving drive-in restaurants.

Doumar's
20th Street at
Monticello Avenue /
Norfolk / 23502
757-627-4163

This place uses the same cone-making machine designed by the owner's great-uncle in 1905. Doumar's dishes out toasted, hand-rolled wafer ice-cream cones in six homemade flavors. Gourmet magazine cites its ice cream as being among the best in the nation. Order a pork barbecue sandwich to round out your meal.

Wright's Dairy Rite
346 Greenville
Avenue, US 11 /
Staunton / 24401
540-886-0435

This authentic 1950s drive-in (it opened for business in 1952) offers inside and carhop service and classic burgers, fries, and shakes.

Buck's Drive-In
State Route 91 /
Saltville / 24370
276-496-7231

Buck's is famous for its footlong hot dogs.

Speaking of nostalgic places to eat, the next time you're in Culpeper, stop by Gayheart's Drugstore and Soda Fountain at 101 East Davis Street and order an old-fashioned ice-cream soda. In Front Royal, the Royal Dairy offers a variety of ice-cream treats (remember banana splits?) as well as burgers, etc., in its original 1947 building at 241 Chester Street.

La Bergerie
218 North Lee Street / Alexandria / 22314-2688
703-683-1007

This French restaurant near the waterfront is a longtime Old Town favorite that offers traditional décor and top-rate food and service.

Le Gaulois
1106 King Street / Alexandria /   22314
703-739-9494

Whether you eat in one of the wood-beamed, copper-pot-decorated dining rooms or outside on the garden patio, you'll surely enjoy the wonderful country French food here, long one of the best values in Old Town.

Elysium
Morrison House, 116 South Alfred Street / Alexandria /
22314
800-367-0800 or 703-838-8000
www.morrisonhouse.com

You don't get a menu at this innovative Old Town restaurant. Instead, the chef comes to your table, describes the fresh ingredients he is featuring that day, and then prepares a meal based on your desires and preferences. Reservations are a must.

Four & Twenty Blackbirds
650-A Zachary Taylor Highway, State Route 522 / Flint Hill /
22627
540-675-1111

Getting here is half the fun, down curvy country roads and through gorgeous mountain scenery. Housed in an old general store, this restaurant is slightly funky, thanks to the walls and trim painted green and pink and the poster-sized Audubon bird prints on the walls. The seasonal menu changes frequently, but the yummy homemade breads and biscuits served before meals never change, thankfully. Four & Twenty Blackbirds offers Sunday brunch and dinner Wednesday through Saturday.

Inn at Little Washington
Middle and Main Streets / Washington / 22747
540-675-3800
www.relaischateaux.com (use the search feature)

The owners of this inn, located about an hour's drive west of the Washington, D.C., suburbs, like to say that this is the first Five-Star, Five-Diamond inn in America, and deservedly so. The Inn at Little Washington is the place to go for a truly unforgettable evening. You might even spot a politician or a movie star or other celebrity (Federal Reserve chief Alan Greenspan and newswoman Andrea Mitchell were married here a few years back). The service is friendly and the food is some of the best anywhere. It is quite expensive, though, and you must reserve well ahead of time.

The Trick Dog Café
4357 Irvington Road / Irvington / 22480
804-438-1055
www.trickdogcafe.com

Located near the Hope and Glory Inn (see page 205), the Trick Dog Café serves bistro food and a wide selection of wines in a cozy setting (think white picket fence). It is frequently cited as one of the best places for dinner in the Northern Neck.

The Trellis Café
403 Duke of Gloucester Street / Williamsburg / 23185
757-229-8610
www.thetrellis.com

Some of the best food and wine in Virginia can be found at the Trellis. This is a great place to enjoy lunch (you can sit in the outdoor café right in the heart of the historic district) or have a romantic evening meal. The chef/owner is the author of *Death by Chocolate* and other dessert cookbooks, so don't plan on skipping dessert.

The Dining Room at Ford's Colony
240 Ford's Colony Drive / Williamsburg / 23188
757-258-4107
www.fordscolony.com

Located on the grounds of a country club, this restaurant—open to the public—is a special-occasion kind of place. It's dressy and elegant, with 18th-century décor and waiters in formal attire. You can count on great food and wine.

Todd Jurich's Bistro
210 York Street / Norfolk / 23510
757-622-3210

This is probably the least touristy and most romantic dining spot in downtown Norfolk. The food is creative, consistently good, and enticingly prepared; the desserts are sinful.

Omar's Carriage House
313 West Bute Street / Norfolk / 23510
757-622-4990

h i g h l i g h t

Chocolate Heaven

If your idea of romance involves giving or receiving sinfully delicious chocolates, then don't miss the Cocoa Mill Chocolate Company at 115 West Nelson Street in downtown Lexington. The shop gained national fame awhile back when the Wall Street Journal *named its chocolates the best in the country. The truffles—which the* Journal *described as "dense, slightly crumbly and in grown-up flavors like Grand Marnier and cappuccino, not overly sweet"—are a specialty. For more information, dial 800-421-6220 or visit www.cocoamill.com.*

This small, friendly, downtown favorite near the YMCA is noted for its wonderful contemporary American cuisine. The emphasis here is on seafood thoughtfully prepared and well priced. The upstairs dining room is a little quieter than the downstairs. Omar's is open for lunch, dinner, and Sunday brunch.

**Alexander's on the Bay
  Restaurant
  536 Ocean View Avenue (at the
  foot of Fentress Avenue) /
  Virginia Beach / 23455
  757-464-4999
  www.alexandersonthebay.com**

The view of the Chesapeake Bay and the bridge-tunnel from this upscale beach-side restaurant (admittedly a little off the beaten path) makes it one of the most romantic dining spots in Virginia Beach. Seafood is the specialty, but Angus beef dishes (how about Châteaubriand for two?) are also served. An extensive wine list is offered.

**Il Giardino Ristorante
910 Atlantic Avenue / Virginia   Beach / 23451
757-422-6464
www.ilgiardino.com**

This longtime oceanfront favorite features foccacia and

pizza baked in an Italian wood-burning oven, along with classic fish, veal, chicken, and pasta dishes. A piano bar and dance floor let you make an evening of your visit here. *Wine Spectator* magazine has included Il Giardino in its annual ratings of restaurants with outstanding wine lists.

It's About Thyme
128 East Davis Street / Culpeper   / 22701
580-825-4264

It's not always easy to find good restaurants in small Virginia towns, but this one in an old store in downtown Culpeper is a winner for both lunch and dinner. With huge, hand-painted murals of Italian scenes on the walls, it specializes in country European cuisine. The choices are varied (from pasta to pot roast), innovative, and tasty. You can also choose from a nice wine selection and an array of tempting desserts.

Claiborne's
200 Lafayette Boulevard / Fredericksburg / 22401
540-371-7080
www.claibornesrestaurant.com

At Claiborne's, Southern low-country and traditional American food are served in an elegant setting—a transformed historic train depot in downtown Fredericksburg.

Bistro 309
309 William Street / Fredericksburg / 22401
540-371-9999
www.bistro309.com

The menu changes with the seasons at Bistro 309. The food in this lovely white-tablecloth restaurant is cooked with a Southern accent. The works of local artists are featured in changing exhibits on the dining-room walls.

Palladio
17655 Winery Road / Barboursville / 22923
540-832-7848
www.palladiorestaurant.com

Lunch and dinner at this authentic northern Italian restaurant at Barboursville Vineyards are almost as enjoyable as a trip to Italy. The staff is Italian, and the food is top rate, if pricey (take a look at sample menus on the website). The winery is owned by a large Italian wine company, Zonin.

Métropolitain
214 West Water Street / Charlottesville / 22902
434-977-1043

There are several very good dinner restaurants in downtown Charlottesville. This French spot always get high ratings and is near the downtown walking mall.

C&O Restaurant
515 East Water Street / Charlottesville / 22902
434-971-7044

The C&O, located across the street from the old train station, is a longtime Charlottesville favorite for its innovative country-French-influenced menu. For a romantic evening, request a table in the quiet upstairs dining room.

Ivy Inn
2244 Old Ivy Road / Charlottesville / 22903
434-977-1222
www.ivyinnrestaurant.com

This secluded, two-centuries-old house is one of the most romantic spots to dine in Charlottesville. It offers several intimate dining rooms throughout the house and a tented garden patio in the warm months. William Faulkner once owned the estate on which this house sits.

Clifton: The Country Inn
1296 Clifton Inn Drive / Charlottesville / 22911
888-971-1800 or 434-971-1800
www.cliftoninn.com

The restaurant here is as highly regarded as the inn (see pages 209-10). It's open to the public, but you must make reservations early if you want to experience the great food and atmosphere. Before dinner, guests are invited into the drawing room, where cocktails and complimentary appetizers are served and the chef describes the meal to come. The menu is fixed-price; your only decision is the entrée—fish or meat.

Amici Ristorante
3343 West Cary Street / Richmond / 23221
804-353-4700

Located in the fun and funky Carytown district, this charming, authentic northern Italian restaurant serves consistently good food, including homemade pastas. Patio seating is available.

Lemaire
Jefferson Hotel, 101 West Franklin Street / Richmond /
23219
804-649-4644
www.jefferson-hotel.com

Lemaire is one of just 36 restaurants in the country to receive AAA's Five Diamond designation. Dining in this downtown classic is simply exquisite.

Zeus Gallery Café
201 North Belmont Avenue / Richmond / 23221
804-359-3219

Not far from Carytown, this small, out-of-the-way restaurant specializes in seafood and vegetarian dishes.

Dining Room at the Berkeley
Berkeley Hotel, 12th and Cary Streets / Richmond / 23219
804-780-1300
www.berkeleyhotel.com

Consistently rated one of the best and most romantic restaurants in Richmond—and in the state—this Shockoe Slip establishment features Virginia products on its menu.

Violino Ristorante Italiano
181 North Loudoun Street / Winchester / 22601
540-667-8006

Violino, owned by a couple from Turin, Italy, serves authentic northern Italian food and good wine in a romantically musical setting at the northern end of the Old Town pedestrian mall.

L'Auberge Provençale
P.O. Box 190 / White Post / 22663
800-638-1702 or 540-837-1375
www.laubergeprovencale.com

This combination romantic inn and restaurant occupies a

1753 stone house alongside US 340 in the Shenandoah Valley not far from Leesburg and Winchester. French and American classics are served in several beautifully (but not stuffily) decorated rooms.

Joshua Wilton House
412 South Main Street / Harrisonburg / 22801
540-434-4464
www.joshuawilton.com

This restaurant, part of an inn in a beautifully restored Victorian house, offers some of the best dining for miles around. Meals featuring fresh, local farm products are served in five intimate dining rooms on the main floor of the inn and on a tree-shaded outdoor patio in the summer months.

Bell Grae Inn and Restaurant
515 West Frederick Street / Staunton / 24401
888-541-5151 or 540-886-5151
www.bellegrae.com

Southern food with a modern twist and a nice selection of wines from Virginia and elsewhere are served in the elegant dining rooms and the indoor-outdoor Garden Room at this Italianate Victorian inn. Dinners are fixed-price; lunch is served by advance notice to groups only.

Willson-Walker House
30 North Main Street / Lexington / 24450
540-463-3020

Southern-style American cuisine is served in Lexington's most romantic and reliable downtown restaurant. The menu changes frequently at the Willson-Walker House. Ask about the

Theater at Lime Kiln dinner package on Wednesdays. The restaurant is open for lunch and dinner.

 The Southern Inn
37 South Main Street / Lexington / 24450
540-463-3612
www.southerninn.com

Offering foods made with locally grown products and homemade baked goods, the Southern Inn has been a fixture in downtown Lexington since 1932. Of course, the menu has changed quite a bit over the years, and in fact still does, depending on the season. The chef is a frequent participant in chef's dinners at wineries. His wine list reflects an emphasis on pairing good food with good wines.

 Maple Hall
3111 North Lee Highway, US 11 / Lexington / 24450
877-463-2044 or 540-463-4666

The restaurant in Maple Hall, a country inn in a Civil War-era mansion just a few minutes north of Lexington, has been popular with the locals for special occasions for years.

 Carlos Brazilian International Cuisine
4167 Electric Road / Roanoke / 20414
540-776-1117

This eclectic restaurant, long a Roanoke favorite, has moved to a new location from its original downtown spot across from the farmers' market. It features foods from Brazil, Italy, and France and is regularly cited as being the best dining experience in the area.

Regency Dining Room
Hotel Roanoke and Conference Center,
   110 Shenandoah Avenue / Roanoke / 24016
540-985-5900
www.hotelroanoke.com

This elegant 1880s Tudor-style hotel in the downtown area has been completely refurbished. Its elegant dining room, although expensive, is the most romantic spot in the city.

Oddfellas Cantina
110-A North Locust Street / Floyd / 24091
540-745-3463
www.oddfellascantina.com

You won't find white linen tablecloths and candelabras in this town. Floyd is all about music, and this restaurant—which features quality Southwestern-influenced cuisine prepared with local produce, as well as breads baked in a wood-fired oven— is a town favorite for all kinds of singing and playing, from Irish to old-time to jazz. Call or check Oddfellas' website for the schedule.

The Dining Room at Camberley's Martha Washington Inn
150 West Main Street / Abingdon / 24210
276-628-3161
www.camberleyhotels.com

Probably the most elegant dining in southwestern Virginia is found in this historic hotel dining room. The Sunday brunch is especially popular with the locals.

▲▲ **The Tavern**
222 East Main Street / Abingdon / 24210
276-628-1118

Constructed in 1779, Abingdon's oldest building is also one of the oldest in the Blue Ridge. Today, it houses a restaurant featuring the foods and wines of Virginia and Europe. One of the owners is German. The couple also runs a gourmet shop at 130 Pecan Street, near the entrance to the Virginia Creeper Trail; there, you can buy all sorts of gourmet food items, including wines, beers, and cheeses, or even rent a bike to take out on the trail.

Romantic Getaway

THE BLUE RIDGE FOOTHILLS— WARRENTON, CULPEPER, SPERRYVILLE, FRONT ROYAL

This area is a popular day trip and weekend getaway for couples from the Washington, D.C., metropolitan area, since it's only about an hour's drive west. In fact, at the height of the peak fall leaf season, Skyline Drive looks more like the Beltway, so it's best to plan a trip to Shenandoah National Park for some other time. Outdoor activities are the area's big draw. Floating down the river, hiking, waterfall watching, and bicycling lead the way, followed by back-roads driving, winery hopping, and antique hunting.

THINGS TO DO

♥ Tube or canoe on the Shenandoah River (see pages 89-90)
♥ On your way to Skyline Drive, stop in the village of Sperryville for

a unique shopping experience, in particular at the Sperryville Emporium, at the glass-blowing studio, at the catalog outlet store, at the handcrafted furniture place with a sign that reads "Antiques Made Daily," and at the great little bookstore housed in a converted church

♥ Climb to the top of Old Rag Mountain or hike to a waterfall in Shenandoah National Park (see pages 58, 62, and 88)

♥ Sample dozens of wines at one of two Virginia wine festivals held yearly at Great Meadows (see pages 38-39)

♥ Watch steeplechase races at the Virginia Gold Cup (see page 112)

♥ Have a light lunch on Linden Vineyard's expansive deck overlooking the vineyards and orchards (see pages 181-82)

♥ Skim over valleys and mountaintops in a hot-air balloon (see pages 95-96)

♥ Shop for fresh organic produce, eggs, and beef at Sunnyside Farms in Little Washington (see page 191)

♥ Watch stunt-flying biplanes at the Flying Circus Airshow in Bealeton (see page 94)

♥ Shop for gifts and antiques in the Old Town areas of Culpeper, Front Royal, and Warrenton

♥ Grab a picnic lunch or dinner and a bottle of wine at J's Gourmet in Front Royal (see below)

PLACES TO EAT

♥ It's About Thyme / Culpeper (see pages 169)

♥ Ashby Inn and Restaurant / Paris (see pages 200-201)

♥ The Inn at Little Washington (see page 166)

♥ Four & Twenty Blackbirds / Flint Hill (see pages 165-66)

♥ Flint Hill Public House / State Route 522 / Flint Hill / 22627; 540-675-1700

♥ J's Gourmet / 206 South Royal Street / Front Royal / 22630; 540-636-9293

♥ Old Town Café / 79 Main Street / Warrenton / 20186; 540-347-4147

♥ Rae's Place and Deli / 12018-A Lee Highway / Sperryville / 22740; 540-987-9733

PLACES TO STAY

♥ Skyland Lodge and Big Meadows Lodge / Shenandoah National Park (see pages 215-16)
♥ The Inn at Meander Plantation / Locust Grove (see page 209)
♥ Ashby Inn and Restaurant / Paris (see pages 200-201)
♥ Chester House Bed and Breakfast / Front Royal (see page 215)
♥ Middleton Inn / Washington (see page 203)
♥ The Inn at Little Washington (see page 166)
♥ Caledonia Farm-1812 / Flint Hill (see pages 202-3)
♥ Belle Meade Bed and Breakfast Inn / Sperryville (see page 203)
♥ The Inn at Fairfield Farm / Hume (see page 202)

FOR MORE INFORMATION

♥ Front Royal/Warren County Chamber of Commerce / 414 East Main Street / Front Royal / 22630; 540-635-3185; www.frontroyalchamber.com
♥ Fauquier County Chamber of Commerce / 183A Keith Street, P.O. Box 127 / Warrenton / 20188; 540-347-4414; www.fauquierchamber.org
♥ Culpeper Department of Tourism / 109 South Commerce Street / Culpeper / 22701; 888-CULPEPER, 540-825-8628 (visitor center), or 540-727-0611; www.visitculpeperva.com

COOKING CLASSES

Learning new things to cook together can be a different, fun, and practical thing to do. Some of the places listed below are inns or bed-and-breakfasts that let you make a weekend of it, while others are regular schools offering night and weekend classes. The best part is that you get to eat what you've prepared. See the websites listed, or call for details.

Lansdowne Resort and Conference Center
44050 Woodridge Parkway / Leesburg / 20176
800-541-4801 or 703-858-2107
www.lansdowneresort.com/culinary.html

L'Auberge Chez François/Jacques Haeringer
332 Springvale Road, P.O. Box 674 / Great Falls / 22066
703-759-3800
www.chefjacques.com

Stratford University's Culinary Workshops
7777 Leesburg Pike / Falls Church / 22043
703-734-5307
44050 Woodridge Parkway / Leesburg / 20176
703-858-2107
www.stratford.edu/culinaryclasses.html

Judy Harris Cooking School
2402 Nordok Place / Alexandria / 22306
703-768-3767
www.judyharris.com

A Pinch of Thyme Cooking School
308 South Payne Street / Alexandria / 22314
703-683-5034
www.robynwebb.com

Channel Bass Inn
6228 Church Street / Chincoteague Island / 23336
800-249-0818 or 804-336-6148
www.channelbass-inn.com

The Inn at Meander Plantation
HCR 5, Box 460 / Locust Dale / 22948
800-385-4936 or 540-672-4912
www.meander.net

Boar's Head Inn Country Resort
200 Ednam Drive / Charlottesville / 22903
800-476-1988 or 434-296-2181
www.boarsheadinn.com

Helen Worth's Culinary Instruction
1701 Owensville Road / Charlottesville / 22901
434-296-4380

The Seasonal Cook
218 West Water Street / Charlottesville / 22902
434-295-9355

The Compleat Gourmet
3030 West Cary Street / Richmond / 23221
804-353-9606
www.thecompleatgourmet.com/classes.htm

Terra Cotta Kitchen
Creekside Station, 3031 Valley Avenue, US 11 / Winchester /
22601
540-723-8800
www.terracottakitchen.com

L'Auberge Provençale Bed and Breakfast and Restaurant
P.O. Box 190 / White Post / 22663
800-638-1702 or 540-837-1375

Wade's Mill
55 Kennedy-Wade's Mill Loop / Raphine / 24472
800-290-1400 or 540-348-1400
www.wadesmill.com

WINERIES

Here's a short list of Virginia's most romantic wineries. All of those listed have at least one wine considered by *Wine Spec-*

tator magazine to be among the best in the South.

For a brochure describing the 60-plus wineries in the state and a calendar of wine festivals and events, contact the Virginia Wine Marketing Program, P.O. Box 1163 / Richmond / 23218. You can receive information by dialing 800-828-4637 or by visiting www.virginiawines.org.

For a listing of selected Virginia wine festivals, see pages 37-44.

Breaux Vineyards
36888 Breaux Vineyards Lane / Hillsboro / 20132
800-492-9961 or 540-668-6299
www.breauxvineyards.com

This classy winery west of Leesburg is just a few years old but is already gaining national recognition. It specializes in whites, though its Merlot has been highly rated by *Wine Spectator*. After visiting the Mediterranean-style tasting room, you can step outside to the Patio Madeleine, order a glass of Breaux wine, cheese, and fresh-baked French bread, and gaze across the manicured grounds for a great view of the Blue Ridge Mountains.

Linden Vineyards
3708 Harrels Corner Road / Linden / 22642
540-364-1997
www.lindenvineyards.com

Linden, located a few miles down a curvy country lane off I-66 east of Front Royal, is, to put it simply, a rare treat. The rustic winery and tasting room are snuggled into a scenic spot in the Blue Ridge foothills. A large deck offers picture-perfect views of sloping vineyards, orchards, and blueberry bushes. On that deck—part of which can be enclosed with huge glass doors in the cool months—you can order warm baguettes, locally made cheeses, and Virginia sausage, along with a glass of one of Linden's very good wines. In 2002, *Wine Spectator* gave a Linden red and a Linden white its highest ratings for Virginia wines. Barrel tastings, winemaker's dinners, and other food events take place throughout the year, but be sure to book early.

Oasis Winery
14141 Hume Road / Hume / 22639
800-304-7656 or 540-635-7627
www.oasiswine.com

Oasis is perhaps a bit too commercial to be called romantic, but its mountain setting draws people from the nearby Washington, D.C., area year-round to sample the highly rated white wines and sparkling wines and to enjoy the heated outdoor deck and pavilion and the lunch café. Weddings can be held here.

Ingleside Plantation Vineyards
5872 Leedstown Road / Oak Grove / 22443
804-224-8687
www.ipwine.com

Located in the Northern Neck about 30 miles south of Fredericksburg, Ingleside is one of the state's oldest vineyards. Its Chardonnays have won several state awards and a *Wine Spectator* rating. Weddings are held in the European-style courtyard.

Barboursville Vineyards
17655 Winery Road / Barboursville / 22923
540-832-3824
www.barboursvillewine.com

Barboursville produces some of the most respected wines in the state. Its peaceful rural setting in the Virginia Piedmont north of Charlottesville makes the Italian-looking winery—now owned by a large Italian wine company—a great day-trip destination. On the grounds are two unforgettable attractions in addition to the winery's rustic tasting room: the ruins of a large brick mansion designed by Thomas Jefferson for a former Virginia governor, and an authentic Italian restaurant, Palladio, that will make you think you're in northern Italy. The winery offers a full schedule of events year-round, including guest-chef dinners, barrel tastings, Virginia Opera performances, and Shakespeare performed outdoors with the Barboursville ruins as a backdrop.

Jefferson Vineyards
1353 Jefferson Parkway / Charlottesville / 22902
800-272-3042 or 434-977-3042
www.jeffersonvineyards.com

Jefferson's red wines have garnered even more awards than its whites, unusual for a Virginia winery. The winery and tasting room sit under a grove of sycamore trees in a rural location. You're encouraged to bring a picnic lunch (which you can buy at Brix Marketplace, near the entrance to the winery) to eat on the deck; you can then buy a glass of wine to accompany lunch and enjoy the free mountain views. The grapes are grown right here, on the same land where Thomas Jefferson encouraged an Italian winemaker to plant vines more than two centuries ago.

highlight

*Valentine's Day
Celebrations at
Virginia Wineries*

Here's a romantic idea for Valentine's Day: Have dinner or taste wine and chocolates at one of the many wineries in the state that put on special events for the occasion. The wineries below have sponsored such functions in past years; call for current information.

Breaux Vineyards
36888 Breaux Vineyards
Lane / Hillsboro /
20132
800-492-9961 or 540-
668-6299
www.breauxvineyards.com
Breaux, west of Leesburg, celebrates the day with its Valentine's Chocolate and Cabernet Weekend.

Tarara
13648 Tarara Lane /
Leesburg / 20176
703-771-7100
www.tarara.com

Tarara hosts a five-course Valentine's Day dinner and a brunch.

Willowcroft Farm
Vineyards
38906 Mount Gilead
Road / Leesburg /
20175
703-777-8161
www.willowcroftwine.com
Willowcroft offers a red wine and chocolate tasting.

Oasis
14141 Hume Road /
Hume / 22639
800-304-7656 or 540-635-
7627
www.oasiswine.com
Visitors can sample the highly rated Oasis champagne and wine-filled chocolates by the winery's romantic fireplace.

Gray Ghost
Vineyards
14706 Lee Highway /
Amissville / 20106
540-937-4869
This winery's annual celebration features chocolate desserts and Cabernet.

Blue Ridge WineWay
Valentine's Weekend
800-820-1021
www.blueridgewineway.com
Eight wineries sponsor a progressive wine journey with food and entertainment on the Blue Ridge WineWay.

Windy River Winery
20268 Teman Road /
Beaverdam / 23015
804-449-6996
www.windyriverwinery.com

Windy River's "Roué and Chocolates" event features live violin music.

Prince Michel and
Rapidan River Vineyards
HCR 4, Box 77 / Leon /
22725
540-547-3707
www.princemichel.com

This winery is located on US 29 nine miles south of Culpeper. You can taste the Prince's Virginia sparkling wine with chocolates on or around Valentine's Day or have dinner in the romantic restaurant.

Barboursville
Vineyards
17655 Winery Road /
Barboursville / 22923
540-832-3824
www.barboursvillewine.com

Visitors celebrate the day with a wine tasting and dessert sampling from the winery's Palladio Restaurant.

Stonewall Vineyards
Route 2, Box 107A /
Concord / 24538
434-993-2185
www.stonewallwine.com

Lovers come to dine and dance at Stonewall's Wine and Roses Valentine's Dinner.

North Mountain
Vineyard and Winery
4374 Swartz Road /
Maurertown / 22644
540-436-9463
www.northmountainvineyard.com

North Mountain hosts a catered winemaker's dinner, as well as a free wine and chocolate tasting, on the weekend closest to Valentine's Day.

Shenandoah Vineyards
3659 South Ox Road /
Edinburg / 22824
540-984-8699
www.shentel.net/shenvine

Visitors enjoy a candlelight Valentine's dinner with wine pairings.

Château Morrisette
P.O. Box 766 / Meadows
of Dan / 24120
540-593-2865
www.thedogs.com

This Blue Ridge Parkway winery puts on its Valentine's Day Puppy Love Dinner in its restaurant.

Rockbridge Winery
30 Hill View Lane / Raphine / 24472
888-511-WINE
www.rockbridgewine.com

This Shenandoah Valley winery's Merlot is a Governor's Cup Gold Award winner. Its whites have received numerous awards as well. Located not far off I-81 about 18 miles north of Lexington, this friendly country winery is housed in an old red barn. It's quite laid-back and rustic.

Valhalla Vineyards
6500 Mount Chestnut Road / Roanoke / 24018
540-725-WINE
www.valhallawines.com

Valhalla's 1999 Syrah was rated among the best in Virginia (and the South) by *Wine Spectator*. The magazine also had kind words for two other Valhalla reds and a white. The winery hosts special events throughout the year, but lovers shouldn't miss the annual Valentine's Chocolate and Wine Celebration.

Villa Appalaccia Winery
752 Rock Castle Gorge (off the Blue Ridge Parkway) /
**   Floyd / 24091**
540-593-3100
www.villaappalaccia.com

If you're driving on the Blue Ridge Parkway near Milepost 170 and you see what appears to be a Tuscan farmhouse flying the Italian flag, you aren't hallucinating. This is the home of a relatively new Virginia winery, Villa Appalaccia. Its excellent wines—mostly reds—are inspired by the wines of northern Italy. The views are spectacular. Who'd think grapes would grow so well in these high mountains? They're even trying to grow olive trees here! The winemaker commutes; she's a professor at a university in North Carolina, and her husband, a retired academic, runs the operation. One of Villa Appalaccia's wines has already won a Governor's Cup Gold Award, and its Pinot Grigio has been rated by *Wine Spectator*.

PICK YOUR OWN FRUITS AND VEGETABLES

Farmers' markets and roadside stands can be found all over Virginia in the summer and early fall. They're great places to buy fresh fruits, vegetables, cheeses, apple cider, baked goods, and homemade jams. But there's another option: pick your own. Although it requires a little more work on your part, it can be fun, and you're guaranteed freshness. Be sure to bring containers and to call first to verify that the crop is in.

The Virginia Department of Agriculture and Consumer Services publishes the annual *Virginia Grown Guide to Pick-Your-Own and Select-Your-Own Virginia Farm Products*, which lists farmers in Virginia who market directly to consumers and also lists farmers' markets statewide. You can get a free copy by visiting www.vdacs.state.va.us/vagrown, by writing VDACS, P.O. Box 1163 / Richmond / 23218, or by calling 804-786-5867.

Below are a few pick-your-own places from the guide to give you an idea of the types of produce available.

Crooked Run Orchard
37883 East Main Street / Purcellville / 20132
540-338-6642

Visitors come here for strawberries (late May to mid-June),

h i g h l i g h t

Recipe for a
Romantic Picnic: A Loaf of Bread,
a Jug of Virginia Wine, and a Chunk of Virginia

If your travels take you into the Virginia countryside, away (thankfully) from fast-food places and city restaurants, consider packing a simple picnic lunch. All you need is some fresh, crusty bread, a bottle of Virginia wine, fresh fruit from a roadside stand, and a chunk of cheese made in the state.

There are several excellent cheesemakers in Virginia. Many sell their products in area gourmet shops and wine stores, while some have retail shops on their premises. All will fill orders by mail. Here are six:

Blue Ridge Mountain Dairy
12745 Milltown Road / Lovettsville / 20180
540-822-4363
www.blueridgedairy.com

This dairy offers farmhouse mozzarella, applewood-smoked mozzarella, fresh whey ricotta, mascarpone, and mozzarella rolls with prosciutto, sun-dried tomato, and basil pesto. It has no retail shop but does accept mail orders.

Tack House Kitchen and Creamery
P.O. Box 423 / Flint Hill / 22627
540-675-3444

Tack House produces fresh and aged goat cheeses, including Feel Good Cheese, Jordan River Chevre, Herbs de Provence, Mariam Bleu, Lavender Bleu, and Rappahannock Tome.

Everona Dairy
23246 Clarks Mountain Road / Rapidan / 22733
540-854-4159

This dairy offers aged sheep's-milk cheese and pepper-and-herb cheese.

WINING AND DINING 189

 Monastery Country Cheese
Our Lady of the Angels Monastery, 3365 Monastery Drive /
   Crozet / 22932
434-823-1452
www.olamonastery.org

Where else can you get Dutch-style Gouda cheese in red wax wheels handmade by Cistercian nuns? Call or visit the monastery's website to request an order form and a brochure.

 Bent-Tree Farm
7995 Wood Drive / Disputanta / 23842
888-GOAT-MLK or 804-991-2121
www.bent-treefarm.com

The specialties here are handcrafted semisoft feta and many varieties of soft chevre. Briar Patch Cheese is made from whole goat's milk. Disputanta is about 35 miles southeast of Richmond.

 Meadow Creek Dairy
6380 Meadow Creek Road / Galax / 24333
276-236-2776
www.meadowcreekdairy.com

This dairy offers a variety of soft, semisoft, and hard farmstead cheeses.

sour cherries (late June to late July), thornless blackberries and peaches (July and August), and apples and pears (beginning in August).

Hartland Orchard
P.O. Box 124 / Markham / 22643
540-364-2316
www.hartlandorchard.com

This orchard offers sweet and sour cherries (June), peaches

(August), and apples, sweet corn, and pumpkins (beginning in August).

 Westmoreland Berry Farm and Orchard
1235 Berry Farm Lane /
   Oak Grove / 22443
800-997-BERRY or 804-224-9171
www.westmorelandberryfarm.com

Visitors can pick strawberries, black raspberries, and red raspberries during June and September. Westmoreland also offers purple raspberries, blueberries, fresh-picked asparagus, sugar peas, blackberries, peaches, and apples.

 Pungo Blueberries, Etc.
3477 Muddy Creek Road / Virginia Beach / 23456
757-721-7434 (field) or 757-468-5204 (home)

Visitors come here in July and August for the thornless blackberries and blueberries.

 **Double B Farms**
28200 Constitution Highway / Rhoadesville / 22542
540-854-4277

This Orange County farm offers strawberries, blackberries, and red raspberries.

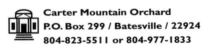 **Carter Mountain Orchard**
P.O. Box 299 / Batesville / 22924
804-823-5511 or 804-977-1833

This orchard produces peaches and nectarines (July), apples (beginning in August), and pumpkins. It is located close to Monticello.

Double "L" Ranch Berry / Grape Farm
State Route 660 / Palmyra / 22963
804-589-4233

Visitors come here for blueberries (June and July), thornless blackberries (mid-June to August), grapes, cherries, and jostaberries (June), and Asian pears (late August).

Marker-Miller Orchards
3035 Cedar Creek Grade / Winchester / 22602
540-662-1391

Marker-Miller offers apricots and Lodi apples (July), peaches (late July to September), green beans, bird egg beans, and tomatoes (July and August), pears (September), and apples and pumpkins (September and October).

Rinker Orchards
1156 Marlboro Road / Stephens City / 22655
540-869-1499

Visitors come here for fresh-picked asparagus (mid-April to mid-June), raspberries (beginning in August), and apples (beginning in mid-August).

Mountain River Gardens
1744 Weyers Cave Road (Exit 235 off I-81) / Grottoes / 24441
540-249-4442

highlight

Organic Delights at Sunnyside Farms

Sunnyside Farms isn't a pick-your-own kind of place, but you can find 60 varieties of organically grown tomatoes, fresh-picked berries, apples, herbs, vegetables, fresh fish such as King Chinook salmon flown in from Alaska (in season, of course), organic Black Angus beef, eggs, and more. It's located at 337 Gay Street in Washington, near Sperryville. For more information, call 540-675-2627 or visit www.sunnysidefarms.com.

This garden offers strawberries and asparagus (May and June).

Crows Nest Farm
1859 Brooksfield Road / Blacksburg / 24060
540-552-4195

Visitors come here for strawberries (late May to mid-June), blueberries (late June to late July), and fall raspberries (early August to October).

---

highlight

Romantic Milk:
The Cream's on Top

There are at least two dairy farms in Virginia where you can buy really fresh milk in glass bottles. (As a Washington Post *feature writer put it, "If you tried to get milk any fresher, the cow would probably slap you.") The milk is pasteurized for safety, but it's left unhomogenized, meaning that the cream floats to the top of the bottle. Don't forget to shake the bottle before pouring.*

Shenville Creamery and Garden Market, in the Shenandoah Valley, sells its own milk, ice cream, soft cheeses, yogurt, and fresh produce. Its farm is off US 211 near New Market at 16094 Evergreen Road / Timberville / 22853. Call 877-600-7440 or 540-896-6357 or visit www.shenville.com.

The other old-fashioned dairy is in the Hampton Roads area. It's Bergey's Dairy Farm, at 2221 Mount Pleasant Road / Chesapeake / 23322. Bergey's offers unhomogenized milk, buttermilk, butter, and ice cream. Call 757-482-4712.

Romantic Getaway

LEESBURG

Although the Leesburg area is fast becoming a Washington, D.C., suburb, the downtown and the surrounding countryside have retained their old-style charm and beauty. Leesburg is one of the state's oldest towns. It's fun to walk around the historic district and admire the many old buildings that have been lovingly restored. There's enough to see and do here to warrant several weekend trips.

THINGS TO DO

- ♥ Shop for unusual gifts and antiques in Leesburg's downtown historic district
- ♥ Take a country drive through the quaint old villages of Hillsboro, Waterford (noted for its October arts and crafts show), Purcellville, and Middleburg (the heart of Virginia hunt country, where Jacqueline Kennedy used to ride horses and Elizabeth Taylor once lived)
- ♥ Shop the upscale boutiques and antique stores in Middleburg
- ♥ In the summer months, check out Loudoun County's many farmers' markets, roadside stands, and pick-your-own farms; take home fresh local produce, home-preserved foods, and cheeses
- ♥ Cut your own fresh bouquet of flowers at Fields of Flowers on State Route 287 near Purcellville
- ♥ Drive south of town to tour beautiful old Oatlands Plantation (see pages 126-27)
- ♥ Watch the sheepdog trials (see page 46) at Oatlands in May
- ♥ Float across the Potomac River to Maryland on one of the last car ferries in Virginia, located at White's Ferry northwest of town

♥ Watch a steeplechase race at Morven Park (see pages 111-12) or in Middleburg (see page 112)

♥ Enjoy music outdoors at one of the many performances of the Bluemont Concert Series (see page 6)

♥ Learn about the cultures of Scotland, Ireland, Wales, and other Celtic nations at the Potomac Celtic Festival (see page 46), held at Morven Park during the second weekend in June

♥ Take in a classical music performance of the Loudoun Symphony (see page 6)

♥ Ride the rapids on the Potomac River in a rental raft, tube, kayak, or canoe from Butt's Tubes in Purcellville (see page 89)

♥ Walk, hike, or bike the Washington and Old Dominion Trail, a 45-mile asphalt trail that runs from Arlington to Purcellville, west of Leesburg

♥ Sample the products of several area wineries, including Breaux Vineyards (see page 181)

♥ Shop for bargains at the upscale Leesburg Corner Premium Outlets

♥ Attend a Sunday-afternoon concert in Waterford (see page 6)

PLACES TO EAT

♥ Lightfoot Restaurant / Leesburg (see page 162)

♥ Tuscarora Mill / 203 Harrison Street SE / Leesburg / 20115; 703-771-9300

♥ Frogs & Friends / 7391 John Marshall Highway / Marshall / 20115; 540-253-5399

♥ Dinner in the Garden / Lovettsville (see page 162)

♥ Ashby Inn / Paris (see pages 200-201)

♥ Black Coffee Bistro / Middleburg (see page 163)

♥ Red Fox Inn / 2 East Washington Street / Middleburg / 20118; 540-687-6301

♥ Coach Stop Restaurant / 9 Washington Street / Middleburg / 20118; 540-687-5515

PLACES TO STAY

♥ Norris House / Leesburg (see page 200)
♥ Ashby Inn / Leesburg (see pages 200-201)
♥ Middleburg Inn and Guest Suites / Middleburg (see page 201)

FOR MORE INFORMATION

♥ Loudoun Tourism Council / 108-D South Street SE / Leesburg / 20175; 800-752-6188; www.visitloudoun.org

Romantic Lodging

*I have found out that there ain't no surer way to find out whether
you like people or hate them than to travel with them.*

Mark Twain

A sure-fire way to put romance back in your life is to
get away from all the things that keep the two of you apart,
like work, household chores, and children. For a true escape,
try spending a night or two alone together in your choice of
romantic Virginia settings: a rustic mountain lodge, an old plantation house, a colonial-era townhouse, a pastel-painted Victorian mansion, a luxurious resort, or a fancy city hotel. Virginia
is full of unique lodging possibilities, and you won't have to
travel far to find a great place.

To my way of thinking, bed-and-breakfasts—especially
those with just a few rooms—offer the most romantic retreats.
Imagine just the two of you, alone at last, sipping wine late
into the night in front of your in-room fireplace in a historic
home or cottage, sleeping late the next morning in a four-poster
bed, and then feasting on a four-course gourmet breakfast. Of
course, hotels offer a little more anonymity and more amenities, such as room service.

The listings below represent just a select few of Virginia's many special places. If you'd like to learn about other lodging statewide, you can receive a free guidebook from the Bed and Breakfast Association of Virginia by writing P.O. Box 1077 / Stanardsville / 22973 or by calling 888-660-BBAV; the organization's website is www.bbav.org. For bed-and-breakfasts in the Shenandoah Valley, go to www.bbhsv.com, the website of Bed and Breakfasts of the Historic Shenandoah Valley.

Norris House Inn
108 Loudoun Street SW / Leesburg / 20175
800-644-1806 or 703-777-1806
www.norrishouse.com

This 1760 stone house has six guest rooms furnished with period antiques and reproductions. It's located in historic downtown Leesburg, near the town's many restaurants and antique and gift shops. The inn's gardens are perfect for a small wedding.

Ashby Inn and Restaurant
692 Federal Street / Paris / 20130
540-592-3900
www.ashbyinn.com

People drive an hour west from the Washington, D.C., area just to come to the Ashby Inn for dinner—it's considered one of the finest dining experiences for miles around. But you can also spend the night in one of the six romantically decorated rooms in this historic 1829 house in tiny Paris. The four larger rooms located in a converted one-room schoolhouse a short stroll from the main house offer privacy and views of the mountains. Country weddings are a specialty of the house (and you can always say you were married in Paris).

Middleburg Inn and Guest Suites
105 West Washington Street / Middleburg / 20118
800-432-6125 or 540-687-3115
www.middleburgonline.com/mgs

You can really spread out in colonial luxury here. This inn offers five suites (meaning bedroom or bedrooms, living room, and kitchen) tastefully furnished with antiques. It's just a short walk to Middleburg's shops and restaurants. The entire inn can be reserved for group get-togethers and special events.

Bailiwick Inn
4023 Chain Bridge Road / Fairfax City / 22030
800-366-7666 or 703-691-2266
www.bailiwickinn.com

This Federal-style inn, located in Old Town Fairfax City across from the county's original courthouse, was built in 1809. Today, it offers 13 rooms and one suite. The inn is a popular spot for weddings and wedding dinners and luncheons, thanks to its romantic restaurant serving French and American cuisine and its lovely brick-walled gardens in back. Guests are asked not to bring their children to the restaurant, a policy that ensures everyone can enjoy an elegant meal in peace.

Morrison House
116 South Alfred Street / Alexandria / 22314
800-367-0800 or 703-838-8000
www.morrisonhouse.com

This elegant "boutique" hotel—rated one of the 10 best in America by at least one national travel magazine—has 42

Birds of a Feather

If you're planning a wedding or other special event within 100 miles or so of the town of Washington, Virginia (in Rappahannock County between Warrenton and Sperryville), consider hiring a flock of doves to provide a different twist to the ceremony. Doves mate for life and have been symbols of peace and love since Roman times.

At the right moment, Cornucopia Farm will release 20 or more doves at your affair. The lovely white birds will circle above the crowd and then head safely home to their loft in Washington, just as they've been trained to do. For details, call Cornucopia Farm at 540-675-2336 or visit www.virginiadoves.com.

not-inexpensive rooms and three suites. Most places to stay in Old Town Alexandria are chain hotels, and they're not cheap either, so the Morrison House is a nice option. It's just two blocks from Old Town's main street and its multitude of shops, galleries, and restaurants.

The Inn at Fairfield Farm
Marriott Ranch, 5305 Marriott
Lane / Hume / 22639
877-324-7344 or 540-364-2627
www.marriottranch.com

The 10 rooms at this inn are scattered among the historic manor house and two other charming structures in the center of the Marriott Ranch, where horseback riding is the activity of choice. Guests here enjoy a Blue Ridge getaway about an hour's drive west of Washington, D.C. Those staying at the inn receive a three-course breakfast and complimentary tea, beer, or wine in the afternoon.

Caledonia Farm-1812
47 Dearing Road / Flint Hill / 22627
800-BNB-1812 or 540-675-3693
http://bnb1812.com

Honeymooners take note. This 1812 historic stone house

nestled into the Blue Ridge Mountains adjacent to Shenandoah National Park has a perfectly private place for you: its Dearing Summer Kitchen, which offers great views, a fireplace, and a hot tub.

Middleton Inn
176 Main Street, P.O. Box 254 / Washington / 22747
800-816-8157
www.middleton-inn.com

If you're planning a romantic dinner at the Inn at Little Washington but shudder at the room rates, consider staying at this nearby bed-and-breakfast. It's not inexpensive, but the Southern ambiance of this 1850 red-brick country mansion may be worth it. The inn is highly rated by several travel publications. It has four rooms with fireplaces and marble baths and a cottage with a full kitchen.

Belle Meade Bed and Breakfast Inn
353 F. T. Valley Road / Sperryville / 22740
540-987-9748
www.bellemeadeinn.com

This old Victorian farmhouse is situated on 138 acres near the charming mountainside village of Sperryville, close to the entrance to Skyline Drive and Shenandoah National Park. It has four rooms with four-poster beds plus the private Comfrey Cottage, which features a deck with Blue Ridge views.

The Garden and Sea Inn
4188 Nelson Road, P.O. Box 275 / New Church / 23415
800-824-0672
www.gardenandseainn.com

Well-tended gardens and an old Victorian house offer a charming respite just a few miles up the road from the bustling town of Chincoteague on Virginia's Eastern Shore. The friendly innkeepers serve delicious meals on weekend nights.

The Inn at Levelfields
10155 Mary Ball Road / Lancaster / 22503
800-238-5578 or 804-435-6887
www.innatlevelfields.com

A long drive leads to this 1800s-era Georgian-style plantation house in the Northern Neck. Antique-filled guest rooms, each with a fireplace, are named by their color—green, red, blue, and yellow. Dinner is served in two formal dining rooms on Friday and Saturday nights. Cooking classes are held here frequently.

Tides Inn
480 King Carter Drive / Irvington / 22480
800-843-3746 or 804-438-5000
www.the-tides.com

The Tides Inn, long a Northern Neck classic, is under new ownership after a multimillion-dollar renovation in 2002. The décor reflects a British colonial motif. Guests here have access to a spa, a golf course, a yacht club where they can rent boats or take a cruise, and classes in wildlife photography and kayaking. Or they can just enjoy the view of Carter Creek (and the Rappahannock River a little farther out) from their balcony or patio. Five restaurants offer a variety of dining experiences, from formal to casual.

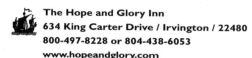

The Hope and Glory Inn
634 King Carter Drive / Irvington / 22480
800-497-8228 or 804-438-6053
www.hopeandglory.com

In addition to the seven whimsically and romantically decorated rooms in the main house—a striking Victorian structure that was once an 1890s schoolhouse—there are four cottages behind the inn, each with a private English garden. Outdoors, guests can plan a late-night rendezvous in the moon garden or take a shower in a secluded claw-foot tub. The Hope and Glory Inn has been written up in travel publications as one of the most romantic places to stay in the country. Weddings, reunions, and other special events can be arranged here.

highlight

Reedville

Several miles north of Irvington is the fishing village of Reedville, a rare sight in this day and age. Here, you can stroll down Main Street to "Millionaire's Row," several colorful Victorian mansions that reflect the town's prosperous past. The Reedville Fishermen's Museum has exhibits about lower Chesapeake watermen, a restored 1875 waterman's home, and a historic boat collection.

From May to mid-October, you can take a day cruise from Reedville across the Chesapeake Bay to Smith Island or Tangier Island. Among the 800 people who live on Tangier Island are some descendants of early English settlers here. The island, located 17 miles east of Reedville, is about one mile wide and three miles long. Golf carts are the primary mode of transportation. Smith Island straddles the Virginia-Maryland line. Like the people of Tangier Island, its residents depend on crabbing, clamming, and fishing for their livelihoods, just as their ancestors did. Many Smith Island citizens are descendants of the Welsh and Cornish settlers of the 1600s, who left Lord Baltimore's colony to establish their own settlements.

Visiting Williamsburg?

A wide range of accommodations is available in Williamsburg. The Colonial Williamsburg Foundation owns and operates seven hotels and inns near the historic area, including the venerable (and pricey) Williamsburg Inn, which has just undergone an extensive renovation. Call 800-HISTORY or visit www.colonialwilliamsburg.com for details and to make reservations.

Inn at Warner Hall
4750 Warner Hall Road /
Gloucester / 23061
800-331-2720 or 804-695-9565
www.warnerhall.com

Truly a part of Virginia history, this white frame 19th-century mansion sits on a Severn River plantation once owned by George Washington's great-great-grandfather. Fixed-price dinners are served in the inn's restaurant. See the website for detailed room descriptions and photos.

Fife & Drum Inn
441 Prince George Street /
Williamsburg / 23185
888-838-1783
www.fifeanddruminn.com

This privately owned bed-and-breakfast is located in the historic district, which makes it convenient for walking to restaurants, shops, William and Mary, and Historic Williamsburg. It has nine rooms tastefully done up in—no surprise—early colonial style.

Kingsmill Resort
1010 Kingsmill Road / Williamsburg / 23185
800-832-5665
www.kingsmill.com

For couples who need a little time apart to make their time together more special, how's this for a romantic weekend? He plays a round of golf on one of Kingsmill's three challenging courses while she signs up for a haircut, a manicure, a pedicure, a facial, a Swedish massage, and a seaweed or paraffin body wrap in the resort's luxurious new spa and fitness center. When his match is over, he can come in for the gentleman's package, which includes a sports facial and a massage. Both partners are sure to be relaxed and ready for a romantic evening.

 Smithfield Inn
112 Main Street / Smithfield / 23430
757-357-1752
www.smithfieldinn.com

The original brick portion of this charming yellow-and-white structure began operation as an inn in 1759. The owners claim that George Washington slept here—really! Today, there are five suites on the second floor above the inn's highly rated restaurant. The inn offers a romantic package that includes champagne, roses, dinner, wine, and even breakfast in bed if you want it. Golf packages are also available. The inn's garden can be reserved for weddings and private parties.

 Smithfield Station
415 South Church Street / Smithfield / 23430
757-357-7700
www.smithfieldstation.com

This inn offers 20 waterfront rooms near the marina on the Pagan River. The most romantic are the two lighthouse suites, in particular the top-level honeymoon suite, which has a two-person shower, a two-person whirlpool tub, a wet bar, a fridge, a fireplace, and a circular staircase leading to an observation cupola.

Bed and Breakfast at the Page House Inn
323 Fairfax Avenue / Norfolk / 23507
800-599-7659 or 757-625-5033
www.pagehouseinn.com

This 100-year-old Georgian Revival mansion in Norfolk's Ghent Historic District was completely restored in 1990 and is now under new ownership. Of the seven lovely rooms, lovers should spring for the Bathe Room, which overlooks the Norfolk skyline and features a fireplace, a tiled sunken tub, and a huge walk-in shower with double showerheads. Don't forget to order a champagne breakfast to be brought to your door.

The Charles Dick House Bed and Breakfast
1107 Princess Anne Street / Fredericksburg / 22401
540-372-6625
www.charlesdickhousebnb.com

This lovely old Southern colonial mansion, built around 1745, is located near the center of town. It is an elegantly restored home with just two large suites, both furnished with antiques and offering large bathrooms.

The Richard Johnston Inn
711 Caroline Street / Fredericksburg / 22401
877-557-0770 or 540-899-7606
www.bbonline.com/va/richardjohnston

Boasting seven rooms and two suites, this historic brick 1700s structure in the heart of Old Town Fredericksburg is an elegant and convenient place to stay. If you want to arrive by train—a truly romantic thing to do in this day and age—it's nice that the inn is just two blocks from the Amtrak station.

The Inn at Meander Plantation
HCR 5, Box 460 / Locust Dale / 22948
800-385-4936 or 540-672-4912
www.meander.net

This 1700s white-columned plantation house on 80 acres in the Blue Ridge foothills is full of Virginia history. Washington, Jefferson, and the Marquis de Lafayette all spent time here. You can even sleep in the same room where Jefferson stayed; he was a friend of the owner and visited often. For a truly romantic stay, consider the Summer Kitchen or one of the three cozy dependencies. Rocking chairs line the huge back porches on both levels, and the Robinson River flows through the property. The inn hosts a series of two-day cooking schools throughout the year. Its gourmet restaurant is open to the public; current menus are posted on the inn's website. Romance packages are available, and weddings can be arranged here.

Willow Grove Inn
14079 Plantation Way / Orange / 22960
800-949-1778 or 540-672-5982
www.willowgroveinn.com

This old plantation house, built around 1778, is painted a lovely shade of yellow and has huge white pillars framing a two-level porch. It offers five private cottages and five rooms or suites in the house. Breakfast and dinner in the inn's fine restaurant are included in the room price.

Clifton: The Country Inn
1296 Clifton Inn Drive / Charlottesville / 22911
888-971-1800 or 434-971-1800
www.cliftoninn.com

This 1799 mansion with tall white pillars and a red roof

once belonged to Thomas Mann Randolph, a Virginia governor and son-in-law of Thomas Jefferson. It was turned into a 14-room inn in 1985 and is now considered one of the best in America. Guests can sip a drink on the veranda and admire the inn's gardens and lawns, filled with huge, old trees. Weddings often take place here. A pool, clay tennis courts, a private lake, and a spa are some of the amenities. The inn's restaurant and wine cellar are also highly rated (see page 171).

The Boar's Head Inn
200 Ednam Drive / Charlottesville / 22903
800-476-1988 or 434-296-2181
www.boarsheadinn.com

This inn sprawls across more than 500 green, manicured acres in the Blue Ridge foothills. There's not much you can't do here. You can get a massage in the spa, play golf, take a cooking class, ride in a hot-air balloon, play tennis (indoors or out), swim, work out, and even have your wedding. The inn, which is owned by the University of Virginia, has 171 rooms, some with fireplaces and balconies. A romance package is available. The Old Mill Room restaurant uses fresh local products and serves up imaginative Virginia cuisine.

Inn at Sugar Hollow Farm
P.O. Box 5705 / Charlottesville / 22905
434-823-7086
www.sugarhollow.com

This serene bed-and-breakfast, built in 1995, sits on 70 acres surrounded by mountains and forests. The five rooms are charmingly decorated in a sophisticated country style. The inn is located 15 miles from historic Charlottesville.

Silver Thatch Inn
3001 Hollymead Drive / Charlottesville / 22911
800-261-0720 or 434-978-4686
www.silverthatch.com

The Silver Thatch Inn, now a charming white clapboard house, had its start in 1780 as a log cabin and has slowly been enlarged over the years. Today, it has seven guest rooms and a restaurant that has been cited by *Wine Spectator* magazine for several years running. Romantic getaway packages are offered.

Keswick Hall at Monticello
701 Club Drive / Keswick / 22947
800-274-5391 or 434-979-3440
www.keswick.com

Other than the Inn at Little Washington, Keswick Hall is perhaps the best-known country inn in Virginia. A *Washington Post* travel writer called it the most luxurious inn in the Mid-Atlantic. This elegant Italianate villa was renovated and expanded by Lord Ashley (husband of the late British designer Laura Ashley) several years ago and is now owned by the Orient Express hotel chain. Located outside Charlottesville in the foothills of the Blue Ridge Mountains, the inn looks more European than Virginian. Much of the property is covered by an 18-hole Arnold Palmer golf course, which the hotel overlooks, adding to the lush, green feel of the place. The inn offers 46 rooms and two suites. It also features two upscale restaurants, swimming pools, tennis courts, and a spa. If you're arriving by helicopter, don't worry—there's a landing pad near the inn.

Prospect Hill Plantation
2887 Poindexter Road / Trevilians / 23093
800-277-0844
www.prospecthill.com

When you turn up the drive to this inviting yellow clapboard country home, you'll feel like you're stepping back in time. The main house dates to 1732. It's only a short drive from Monticello and downtown Charlottesville. The inn's 13 rooms (some of them cottages on the tree-filled garden grounds) and wonderfully romantic dining room (with complimentary wine served before dinner) will have you wishing you never had to leave. All the rooms have fireplaces, and some have spa tubs. A swimming pool is on the premises. Prospect Hill provides a beautiful setting for a wedding, which the innkeepers will help arrange. Packages are available.

High Meadows
55 High Meadows Lane / Scottsville / 24590
800-232-1832 or 434-286-2218
www.highmeadows.com

Built in the 1800s, this lovely old farmhouse—a Virginia Historic Landmark—is unique in having its very own vineyard, noted for its Pinot Noir grapes. Here, you'll find seven period-furnished rooms in the main house, three very private carriage houses (with amenities like fireplaces, private hot tubs, sun decks, and two-person showers), a two-room 1920s garden cottage, and a fitness center. Candlelight dinners are served all week in the inn's three intimate dining rooms, but if you really want to be alone, you can order a European supper basket and tote a complete meal—complete with wine, candles, and more—back to your room. Rates include champagne on arrival, wine tasting and hors d'oeuvres, breakfast, and dinner.

The Jefferson Hotel
101 West Franklin Street /
Richmond / 23220
800-424-8014 or 804-788-8000
www.jefferson-hotel.com

For a one-of-a-kind romantic night or weekend in Richmond, this is the place. A few years back, this 100-year-old hotel went through a multimillion-dollar renovation. Now, it is one of just a handful of Five Star hotels in the United States, as rated by the *Mobil Travel Guide*. Its restaurant, Lemaire, serves gourmet Southern dishes and is highly rated by many publications. You can also treat yourself to afternoon tea in the Palm Court and enjoy an elegant Sunday brunch in the Rotunda. Be ready to splurge, though. Romance packages are available.

highlight

Peak Times for Virginia Country Travel

Be sure to reserve lodging well in advance if you're planning a weekend trip to the Virginia mountains in the fall; peak leaf time is usually around mid-October. The same goes for late spring, particularly mid-May to mid-June, when rhododendrons, azaleas, and mountain laurel bloom along Skyline Drive and the Blue Ridge Parkway. Keep in mind that most inns and bed-and-breakfasts usually are not as full during the middle of the week, if you can travel then.

Linden Row Inn
100 East Franklin Street / Richmond / 23219
804-783-7000
www.lindenrowinn.com

This historic hotel, listed with the National Trust for Historic Preservation, was once a row of townhouses built in 1847. It was transformed into a lovely 69-room inn in 1988. Located in Richmond's historic district, the inn retains its high ceilings and other fine, old architectural features. In the back, there's a brick-walled courtyard and garden where Edgar Allen Poe played as a child. Guests enjoy wine and cheese on their arrival and a complimentary continental breakfast; the dining room also serves traditional Southern dinners.

The Berkeley Hotel
1200 East Cary Street / Richmond / 23219
888-780-1300 or 804-780-1300
www.berkeleyhotel.com

This hotel has been a highly rated Richmond tradition since it opened in 1988. Located in historic Shockoe Slip, it's convenient to the State Capitol, the Canal Walk, restaurants, and shops. Its formal restaurant specializes in Virginia and regional cuisine. Weekend packages are available.

Peaks of Otter Lodge
P.O. Box 489 / Bedford / 24523
800-542-5927 or 540-586-1081
www.peaksofotter.com

This rustic-looking but modern 60-room lodge looks out on a lovely lake along the Blue Ridge Parkway at Milepost 86. Trails go every which way, but mostly up. The rooms here are for the romantic-minded only—there are no phones or televisions to distract you. Food is close by; the lodge has two restaurants, one of which offers a nice wine list. The striking National D-Day Memorial (see page 147) is in nearby Bedford, and Thomas Jefferson's octagonal rural retreat, Poplar Forest (see page 136), is also just a short drive away.

The Inn at Vaucluse Spring
140 Vaucluse Spring Lane / Stephens City / 22655
800-869-0525 or 540-869-0200
www.vauclusespring.com

Two D.C.-area couples bought this property 10 miles south of Winchester in 1995 and turned it into one of the finest bed-and-breakfasts in the Shenandoah Valley. It has 12 rooms in three buildings, including the restored 18th-century manor house and the separate Mill House Studio—a great honeymoon spot. Gourmet meals are served to guests only on Saturday nights.

Chester House Bed and Breakfast
43 Chester Street / Front Royal / 22630
800-621-0441
www.chesterhouse.com

Chester House is a beautiful old home full of elegant architectural detailing. It is situated on two garden-filled acres in the heart of Front Royal's historic district. The ultimate lodging here is the Garden Cottage, a very private 1905 two-story structure featuring a living/dining room, a fireplace, a kitchen, a loft bedroom with a skylight, and a whirlpool tub for two. In the main house are five lovely antique-filled rooms.

Skyland Lodge and Big Meadows Lodge
Shenandoah National Park, P.O. Box 727 / Luray / 22835
800-778-2851
www.visitshenandoah.com

These motel-like lodges owned by the National Park Service may not have the décor of a charming inn or bed-and-breakfast, but their setting high on Skyline Drive is most

highlight

Virginia's Switzerland

Highland County, tucked behind three mountain ranges west of Staunton, is the place to go when you really want to get away from civilization—there are more sheep than people here. Its only real town, Monterey, sits in a peaceful valley surrounded by mountains; the only time traffic is backed up at the county's single traffic light is during the Highland Maple Festival in the spring. There are plenty of places to hike, bike, fish, and drive. Check the chamber of commerce website at www.highlandcounty.org for lodging and dining suggestions.

definitely romantic. A range of rooms is available, from cabins to suites. The lodges are not open in the winter months.

**Strathmore House Bed and
Breakfast
658 Wissler Road / Quicksburg /
22847
888-921-6139 or 540-477-4141
www.strathmorehouse.com**

What could be more romantic than passing down a tree-lined country lane and through one of the state's last surviving covered bridges (Meem's Bottom) to find this charming yellow-and-white century-old Victorian farmhouse on the other side? The wraparound porch takes in views of Strathmore's four acres of English gardens perched above the Shenandoah River. The four rooms are lovingly decorated. Strathmore House is just off historic US 11 between Mount Jackson and New Market.

**Joshua Wilton House
412 South Main Street / Harrisonburg / 22801
540-434-4464
www.joshuawilton.com**

Located on US 11 between downtown and the James Madison University campus, the five-room Joshua Wilton House offers the most elegant lodging and dining in the Harrisonburg area. This rosy pink Victorian home has been lovingly renovated and decorated. Dinner is served on the outdoor patio in warm weather. The inn's pastry chef can even create a special wedding cake for you.

The Selby Inn
Main Street / Monterey / 24465
540-468-3234
www.highlandcounty.org/selbyinn

This 100-year-old house sits on Monterey's Main Street, a great place to be during the town's Highland Maple Festival in March or the Hands and Harvest fall foliage festival in October. The proprietor, a Civil War buff who also runs a bed-and-breakfast in Fredericksburg, conducts tours of the local sites and battlefields.

Inn at Keezletown Road Bed and Breakfast
1224 Keezletown Road / Weyers Cave / 24486
800-465-0100 or 540-234-0644
www.keezlinn.com

You'll get a warm welcome at this century-old Victorian house south of Harrisonburg. The inn offers antique-filled rooms, a lush garden, hearty breakfasts, and a country setting just one mile from I-81.

The Sampson Eagon Inn
238 East Beverley Street / Staunton / 24401
800-597-9722
www.eagoninn.com

Five beautifully decorated rooms, all with four-poster beds, occupy this restored 1840s mansion in a lovely downtown Staunton neighborhood. The rates are reasonable and include a full breakfast. The inn is a short walk from the Woodrow Wilson Birthplace and Museum (see page 138) and performances of the Shenandoah Shakespeare Company at the new Blackfriars Playhouse (see page 21).

 Sugar Tree Inn
State Route 56 / Steeles Tavern / 24476
800-377-2197
www.sugartreeinn.com

The log structures that comprise this rustic but comfortable 12-room inn are set deep in the woods a mile off the Blue Ridge Parkway. The location is convenient to both Staunton and Lexington. A country breakfast is included in the room rate. You won't have to go far for a candlelight dinner, either, since a good restaurant is on the premises. The inn is open from March through December.

---

highlight

Honeymoon Special

Back in 1918, Woodrow Wilson, the 28th United States president, and his bride, Edith Bolling, spent their honeymoon in a Virginia hotel that remains a popular honeymoon destination nearly a century later: The Homestead in Hot Springs.

 Fort Lewis Lodge
HCR 3, Box 21A / Millboro /
24460
540-925-2314
www.fortlewislodge.com

This remote mountain retreat west of Staunton and Lexington has a main house with 15 rooms, but the most romantic accommodations are the one-bedroom log cabins, each with a stone fireplace, a porch, a refrigerator, and a coffee maker. An old silo houses three round guest rooms accessed by a spiral staircase. This is a great spot for doing nothing or for hiking, swimming, or kayaking in the Bullpasture River. The lodge closes for the winter at the end of October. Rates include breakfast and dinner, served in a restored gristmill.

The Homestead
US 220, Main Street, P.O. Box 2000 / Hot Springs / 24445
800-838-1766 or 540-839-1766
www.thehomestead.com

The Homestead is one of the nation's oldest mountain mineral springs resorts. The first lodge of that name opened here in 1766. Now a National Historic Landmark, the hotel and its 500-plus rooms were recently renovated and decorated in a style that epitomizes Southern charm and elegance. You can still take the waters here, but there is so much more to do. There are three golf courses and a spa. There are opportunities for horseback riding, for carriage rides, and for skiing, snowboarding, and ice skating in the winter. You can hike and bike on the resort's 15,000 acres. It's also a great place to do nothing but enjoy the mountain views and the wonderful meals in the several restaurants. It's pricey, but special packages are available, and the off-season rates are more affordable.

Stoneridge Bed and Breakfast / Autumn Ridge Cottages
Stoneridge Lane, P.O. Box 38 / Lexington / 24450
800-491-2930 or 540-463-4090
www.bbonline.com/va/stoneridge or
www.autumnridgecottages.com

Stoneridge is a restored 1829 brick mansion located on 36 acres near historic Lexington and its many shops, restaurants,

highlight

An Underground Wedding

If you'd like an outdoor wedding (well, sort of) but don't want to worry about rain, consider holding your ceremony in one of two Virginia caves. The 57-ton Wedding Bell stalactite at Dixie Caverns in Salem (see page 83) makes a perfect wedding backdrop, while the "stalacpipe" organ at Luray Caverns in Luray (see page 83) provides the music for weddings held there.

and museums. Each of the five rooms in the main house is decorated in colonial style. The owners recently opened Autumn Ridge Cottages two miles south of Lexington. These clapboard cabins with porches look rustic on the outside but are modern inside, featuring whirlpool tubs, full kitchens, and fireplace sitting areas.

 The Hotel Roanoke and Conference Center
110 Shenandoah Avenue /
Roanoke / 24016
540-985-5900
www.hotelroanoke.com

Sitting high on a hill east of the downtown area, the Hotel Roanoke boasts Tudor-style architecture that is distinctively different for Virginia. Inside, this grand old dame of the 1880s has been renovated in classic Southern style. It is now operated by the DoubleTree hotel chain. It's a quick walk through a covered glass walkway to the farmers' market, shops, restaurants, theaters, and museums of the downtown area.

Nesselrod on the New Gardens and Guesthouse
7535 Lee Highway / Radford /   24141
540-731-4970
www.nesselrod.com

This four-room bed-and-breakfast is in a Williamsburg-style

home overlooking the New River. Its romantic features include a fireplace in each room, fresh flower arrangements, and heated towel racks. The specialty here is garden weddings, complete with an arched gazebo chapel, an all-white garden, a sophisticated sound system, and a guesthouse for your reception.

 Stonewall Bed and Breakfast
102 Wendi Pate Trail / Floyd /
24091
540-745-2861
www.swva.net/stonewall

Located near Milepost 159 on the Blue Ridge Parkway, this three-level modern log home is convenient to the shops, restaurants, and live music of Floyd. The honeymoon suite has a private entrance, rustic stone and cedar walls, and a wood-burning stove.

Martha Washington Inn
150 West Main Street / Abingdon / 24210
540-628-3161
www.marthawashingtoninn.com

Built as a private residence in 1832, this elegant home has been turned into a beautiful place to stay, full of Southern charm and ambiance. Part of the Camberley international hotel chain, the hotel offers romance packages and a Barter Theatre package.

> ### *highlight*
>
> ## *The Virginia Creeper Trail*
>
> *This popular 34-mile multiuse trail—for hiking, biking, horseback riding, and cross-country skiing—is maintained by the United States Forest Service. It offers dramatic mountain views as it runs along an old railroad bed from Abingdon to the North Carolina border. The trail is part of Mount Rogers National Recreation Area.*

Summerfield Inn Bed and Breakfast
101 West Valley Street / Abingdon / 24210
800-668-5905
www.summerfieldinn.com

This historic-district 1920s home is within walking distance of the Virginia Creeper Trail and the Barter Theatre. It has four rooms in the main house and three rooms in the new carriage house.

SOME VERY ROMANTIC PLACES FOR A WEDDING

Have you always dreamed of being married in a flower-filled garden? How about posing for your wedding pictures on a Scarlett O'Hara-style grand staircase? Many Virginia gardens, historic homes, inns, and bed-and-breakfasts may be rented for weddings. Most have someone who will help you with all the details, right down to ordering your wedding cake. Here are a few listed in this book.

Northern Virginia
Norris House Inn / Leesburg (see page 200)
Oatlands Plantation / Leesburg (see pages 126-27)
Ashby Inn / Paris (see pages 200-201)
Meadowlark Botanical Gardens / Vienna (see page 75)
Bailiwick Inn / Fairfax City (see page 201)
Morrison House / Alexandria (see pages 201-2)
Carlyle House Historic Park / Alexandria (see pages 127-28)
River Farm / Alexandria (see page 75)
Gunston Hall / Alexandria (see page 129)
Oasis Winery / Hume (see page 182)

Eastern Virginia
Ingleside Plantation Vineyards / Oak Grove (see page 182)
The Hope and Glory Inn / Irvington (see page 205)
Sherwood Forest Plantation / Charles City (see pages 129-30)

Smithfield Inn / Smithfield (see page 207)
Norfolk Botanical Gardens / Norfolk (see page 76)

Central Virginia

Inn at Meander Plantation / Locust Dale (see page 209)
Clifton: The Country Inn / Charlottesville (see pages 209-10)
Boar's Head Inn / Charlottesville (see page 210)
Prospect Hill Plantation / Trevilians (see page 212)
Maymont / Richmond (see page 77)
Lewis Ginter Botanical Garden / Richmond (see pages 76-77)
Valentine Museum/Wickham House / Richmond (see pages 145-46)
Edgar Allen Poe Museum / Richmond (see page 146)
Peaks of Otter Lodge / Bedford (see page 214)

The Shenandoah Valley

Glen Burnie Historic House and Gardens / Winchester (see pages 77-78)
Long Branch / Millwood (see page 137)
Hot-air balloon from Virginia Balloons / Basye (see page 95)
Joshua Wilton House / Harrisonburg (see pages 216-17)
Bell Grae Inn / Staunton (see page 173)
Explore Park / Roanoke (see page 63)
The Homestead / Hot Springs (see page 219)

Southwestern Virginia

Nesselrod on the New Gardens and Guesthouse / Radford (see pages 220-21)
Martha Washington Inn / Abingdon (see page 221)

Romantic Getaway

CHARLOTTESVILLE

Charlottesville and its surrounding area have something for everyone—history, art, music, theater, wineries, fine restaurants, luxurious lodging, shopping, and outdoor events and activities. But it is first and foremost Thomas Jefferson's town. It sometimes seems that everything here springs from the state university he created two centuries ago.

THINGS TO DO

- 💜 Do like the tourists and take in everything Jefferson: Monticello (see pages133-34), the Rotunda at the University of Virginia, the UVA campus in general
- 💜 While on campus, visit the University of Virginia Art Museum (see page 27)
- 💜 Head a short ways out of town to see Australian aboriginal paintings and sculpture at the Kluge-Ruhe Aboriginal Art Collection (see page 28)
- 💜 Tour the back roads in a classic convertible sports car—how about a 1957 Austin-Healey?—rented for a day or a weekend from Classic Cars (434-823-4442)
- 💜 Visit two other presidents' homes: Ash Lawn-Highland (see page 134), James Monroe's abode, not far from Monticello, and Montpelier (see pages134-35), home of James Madison, about 35 miles north of town
- 💜 Walk, shop, or ice skate (at the Ice Park, see page 110) on the bustling downtown pedestrian mall
- 💜 View local artists' work a block off the mall at the McGuffey Art Center (see page 30)

- ♥ Attend a University of Virginia football or basketball game (see page 119)
- ♥ Browse the many wonderful used bookstores in town
- ♥ Visit highly rated local wineries like Jefferson Vineyards (see page 183) and Barboursville Winery (see pages 182-83)
- ♥ Drive a stretch of the Blue Ridge Parkway; there's an entrance 22 miles west of town
- ♥ Play golf at Birdwood in Charlottesville or on the Stony Creek course at Wintergreen Resort, both among the top courses in Virginia (see pages 105 and 108-9)
- ♥ Watch horses jump fences at the Foxfield Races (see page 113) or the races at Montpelier (see page 113-14)
- ♥ Visit historic and charming Scottsville on the James River, where you can ride a pole-propelled ferry or rent a canoe (see page 90)
- ♥ Visit Appomattox, where the Civil War ended
- ♥ Hike to lovely Crabtree Falls (see pages 87-88) in nearby Nelson County
- ♥ In the winter, ski, snowboard, or snow tube at nearby Wintergreen Resort (see pages 108-9)

PLACES TO EAT

- ♥ Métropolitain / Charlottesville (see page 170)
- ♥ Ivy Inn / Charlottesville (see page 170-71)
- ♥ C&O Restaurant / Charlottesville (see page 170)
- ♥ Clifton: The Country Inn / Charlottesville (see page 171)
- ♥ Palladio / Barboursville (see page 170)
- ♥ Caffé Bocce / Valley Street / Scottsville / 24590; 434-286-4422

PLACES TO STAY

- ♥ The Boar's Head Inn / Charlottesville (see page 210)
- ♥ Clifton: The Country Inn / Charlottesville (see pages 209-10)

- ♥ Inn at Sugar Hollow Farm / Charlottesville (see page 210)
- ♥ Silver Thatch Inn / Charlottesville (see page 211)
- ♥ Keswick Hall / Keswick (see page 211)
- ♥ Prospect Hill Plantation / Trevilians (see page 212)
- ♥ High Meadows / Scottsville (see pages 212-13)

FOR MORE INFORMATION

- ♥ Charlottesville/Albemarle County Convention and Visitors Bureau / 600 College Drive, P.O. Box 178 / Charlottesville / 22902; 877-386-1102 or 434-977-1783; www.charlottesvilletourism.org

Index